Lean Six Sigma for Managers and Leaders

A quick reference guide for Lean Six Sigma Practitioners

Prof. Dr. Gopal Sivakumar

B.E. (Prod. Engg.), M.E. (Indl. Engg.), Ph.D. (Mech. Engg.), CSSMBB

Table of contents

INTRODUCTION

Have you ever pondered the secret to achieving sustainable and predictable profit growth? Have you ever aspired to transcend the limitations of traditional managerial approaches and unlock the world of systematic improvement? If so, my dear reader, look no further. Allow me to introduce you to the captivating realm of **Lean Six Sigma for Managers and Leaders.**

As you embark on this literary journey, I implore you to don your metaphorical spectacles and view the world of business processes through a captivating new lens. Driven by the teachings of **Dr. Gopal Sivakumar,** a doctorate in mechanical engineering, an MBB-certified Six Sigma practitioner, trainer, coach, and principal consultant, we will unravel the mysteries of DMAIC methodology and explore its profound impact on your managerial prowess.

But first, let me paint a vivid picture for you. Close your eyes and envision yourself standing atop a hill, overlooking a vast landscape of business opportunities. The air is crisp, carrying with it the promise of untapped potential. As a manager, this terrain is your playground, your canvas upon which you can create masterpieces of efficiency, productivity, and profitability. However, like any artist, you require the right tools, techniques, and, most importantly, mindset.

Enter Lean Six Sigma, a methodology that combines the precision of a Swiss watchmaker with the creativity of a painter, resulting in a symphony of systematic improvement. Its origins can be traced back to visionaries such as Frederick Winslow Taylor and Henry Ford during the Industrial Revolution, as they sought to optimize processes and eliminate waste. Nonetheless, it was in the late 20th century that this methodology truly flourished into a thriving discipline.

Now, imagine a bustling factory floor, overwhelmed by chaos. Broken and outdated processes scatter the landscape like remnants of an ancient civilization. Yet, amidst this disorder, a single beam of hope emerges. It is the voice of a manager, armed with Lean Six Sigma tools, who sees beyond the clutter and envisions a future of streamlined efficiency.

As the manager embarks on the DMAIC methodology - Define, Measure, Analyze, Improve, Control - their journey unfolds like a meticulously crafted novel. They commence by defining the problem at hand, and dissecting it with surgical precision until its true essence is revealed. Equipped with data and metrics, they embark on a quest to measure the current state of affairs, leaving no stone unturned in their pursuit of knowledge.

With each step, the manager delves deeper into analysis, scrutinizing the root causes of inefficiency and waste like a skilled detective. Clues are scattered across the landscape, waiting to be discovered and pieced together like fragments of a puzzle. Through statistical analysis and intuitive insights, the truth begins to emerge, guiding the managers toward the path of improvement.

Oh, what a breathtaking path it is. With every improvement initiative, the manager takes on the role of an alchemist, transforming leaden processes into golden opportunities. Through the power of Lean tools such as 5S deployment and Kaizen, the landscape metamorphoses, obstructions are removed, and an environment conducive to growth and success is created.

However, as in any compelling story, there must be a climactic moment - a moment of truth where all the pieces converge. In the realm of Lean Six Sigma, this moment arrives with the implementation of process controls. Just like a conductor leading an orchestra, the manager ensures that the symphony of efficiency plays on, conducting tests and measurements to ensure that the newfound improvements are sustained and the process does not revert to its former state of chaos.

And thus, dear reader, our journey through the world of Lean Six Sigma for Managers draws to a close. But fret not, for the lessons learned and the wisdom gained will remain with you, guiding you as you navigate the ever-changing landscape of business processes.

Take a deep breath, open your eyes, and embark on this adventure with an open mind. Lean Six Sigma for Managers eagerly awaits your presence, ready to inspire and empower you to unlock the untapped potential within your own managerial domain. Are you ready to embark on this grand adventure? Let us set forth, together, towards a future of profitable growth and boundless possibilities.

CHAPTER 1: UNDERSTANDING THE POWER OF LEAN SIX SIGMA IN BUSINESS OPERATIONS

UNDERSTANDING LEAN PRINCIPLES

Lean, as a concept, was originally developed by Toyota in the 1950s, under the name **Toyota Production System (TPS).** This revolutionary approach to manufacturing focused on reducing waste, improving quality, and increasing efficiency. Over time, this methodology has been adopted and adapted by companies across industries and sectors, transforming the way businesses operate.

The first principle of Lean is the elimination of waste. Waste, in the Lean context, refers to any activity that does not add value to the product or service being delivered to the customer. These non-value-added activities are often referred to as the **"seven wastes"** or the **"7 Muda"** They include transportation, inventory, motion, waiting, overproduction, over-processing, and defects.

Defects are any errors or mistakes in the product or service that result in rework or customer dissatisfaction. Overproduction refers to producing more than what is required, leading to excess inventory and wasted resources. Waiting is the idle time that occurs when people or materials are not being used effectively or efficiently. Transportation is the unnecessary movement of materials or products between locations, adding time and cost to the process. Inventory is excess or obsolete stock that ties up capital and takes up space. Motion refers to unnecessary movement or actions that do not contribute to value creation.

By identifying and eliminating these seven wastes, managers can streamline processes, improve efficiency, and deliver products or services with higher quality and shorter lead times. The purpose is to create a flow that is smooth and uninterrupted, with minimal waste and maximum value for the customer. This approach requires a shift in mindset, from seeing waste as inevitable to actively seeking out and eliminating it.

The second principle of Lean is continuous improvement. Known as Kaizen in the Lean world, continuous improvement involves constantly seeking ways to make processes better, faster, and more efficient. This is achieved through a systematic and disciplined approach, using tools and techniques such as the DMAIC (Define, Measure, Analyze, Improve, Control) methodology, root cause analysis, and process mapping.

Continuous improvement is not a one-time event but rather an ongoing journey. It requires a culture of open communication, collaboration, and learning. It encourages employees at all levels to contribute their ideas for improvement and empowers them to take ownership of their work processes. By fostering a culture of continuous improvement, managers can harness the collective creativity and problem-solving skills of their employees, resulting in innovative solutions and sustained success.

The third principle of Lean is respect for people. In Lean thinking, people are considered the most valuable asset of an organization. Recognizing and respecting the skills, knowledge, and experiences of employees is critical for creating a culture of engagement and empowerment. Lean organizations empower their employees to make decisions, take risks, and contribute to continuous improvement efforts. They provide training and development opportunities to enhance skills and create a sense of ownership and pride in the work.

Respect for people also extends to the relationship between employers and employees. It involves open and honest communication, mutual trust and support, and a commitment to work-life balance. Lean organizations promote a culture of inclusivity and teamwork, where everyone's contributions are valued and recognized.

Understanding and implementing Lean principles can significantly benefit managers and organizations in various ways. By eliminating waste, managers can reduce costs, improve efficiency, and enhance customer satisfaction. By embracing continuous improvement, managers can drive innovation, stay ahead of the competition, and adapt to changing market demands. By fostering respect for people, managers can create a positive and engaging work environment, attract and retain top talent, and build strong and lasting relationships with customers and stakeholders.

In conclusion, Lean principles provide managers with a systematic approach to improve their processes, increase productivity, and achieve cost savings. By understanding and applying the concepts of waste elimination, continuous improvement, and respect for people, managers can transform their organizations into highly efficient and customer-centric entities. The journey towards Lean thinking requires commitment, patience, and perseverance, but the rewards are well worth the effort. With Lean principles as their guide, managers can lead their teams to success and achieve sustainable competitive advantage in today's dynamic and challenging business environment.

TERMINOLOGIES IN LEAN

In the world of Lean manufacturing, several terminologies play a crucial role in shaping the mindset and approach towards achieving operational excellence. In this section, we will delve deep into defining these terminologies and understanding their significance in the context of Lean.

Value-Adding Activity: One of the fundamental principles of Lean is to eliminate waste and focus on activities that create value for the customer. A value-adding activity refers to any process or task that directly contributes to meeting customer needs and requirements. It can be a step that transforms raw materials into a finished product or a service that addresses a customer's specific request. Lean organizations strive to streamline their processes and identify value-adding activities while eliminating non-value-adding ones.

Waste: Waste, or "Muda" in Japanese, is anything that does not add value to the product or service from the customer's perspective. Lean organizations recognize eight different types of waste, which are often referred to as the 7 wastes. These include overproduction, waiting, transportation, processing, inventory, motion, defects, and underutilization of human potential. Recognizing and eliminating waste is a central focus of Lean as it helps organizations become more efficient and cost-effective.

Continuous Flow: Continuous flow is a Lean manufacturing principle that emphasizes the smooth and uninterrupted flow of work through a process. It aims to minimize any disruptions or delays that may occur between steps, thereby reducing lead time and improving overall efficiency. By optimizing the flow of work, Lean organizations can achieve a more predictable and consistent production process while eliminating waste such as waiting and overproduction.

Visual Control: In a Lean environment, visual control refers to using visual cues and indicators to monitor the status of processes and identify abnormalities quickly. It involves the use of visual signals, such as color-coding, charts, graphs, or kanban cards, to provide real-time information about the status of operations. Visual control allows teams to identify bottlenecks, track progress, and take corrective actions promptly, leading to increased transparency and accountability.

7 Wastes: The 7 wastes, also known as the seven deadly wastes, are key areas in which organizations tend to experience inefficiencies. As mentioned earlier, these include overproduction, waiting, transportation, overprocessing, inventory, motion, and defects. By identifying and eliminating these wastes, Lean organizations can significantly improve their processes and achieve higher productivity levels.

5S: 5S is a Lean methodology that focuses on organizing and standardizing the workplace to improve efficiency and safety. The five steps of 5S stand for Sort, Set in Order, Shine, Standardize, and Sustain. Sort refers to removing unnecessary items from the workspace, Set in Order involves logically arranging tools and equipment, Shine refers to cleanliness and maintenance, standardize aims to establish consistent processes and procedures, and sustain involves maintaining the improvements made through regular audits and discipline.

Kaizen: Kaizen is a Japanese term that means "continuous improvement." It is a fundamental concept in Lean thinking, emphasizing the incremental and continuous pursuit of excellence. Kaizen involves all employees, from frontline workers to top management, in identifying small improvements that can be implemented daily. This approach fosters a culture of innovation, encourages employee engagement, and enables organizations to make consistent progress toward their goals.

SMED: SMED, which stands for Single-Minute Exchange of Die, is a Lean technique that focuses on reducing the time it takes to change over a machine or process from one product to another. By minimizing changeover time, organizations can increase flexibility, respond to customer demands more quickly, and reduce inventory levels. SMED involves analyzing the changeover process, eliminating non-value-adding activities, and implementing standardization and improvement measures.

KANBAN: KANBAN is a visual signaling system used in Lean manufacturing to manage and control material flow and production. It involves the use of kanban cards or other visual indicators to signal when and how much material should be produced or replenished. KANBAN helps organizations achieve just-in-time production by ensuring that materials are delivered or produced only when needed, reducing waste and improving overall efficiency.

Heijunka: Heijunka, often translated as production leveling or production smoothing, is a Lean technique that aims to achieve a consistent and balanced production schedule. It involves a systematic approach to workload distribution, enabling organizations to meet customer demand while minimizing fluctuations and variations in production. Heijunka helps organizations maintain a stable and predictable workflow, reducing waste and improving the overall efficiency of their processes.

Jidoka: Jidoka, which can be translated as automation with a human touch, is a Lean principle that focuses on building quality into the production process. It involves empowering workers to stop or address abnormalities and defects as they occur, rather than allowing them to continue downstream. Jidoka emphasizes the importance of taking immediate action to resolve issues and prevent further defects, ensuring that only quality products are passed along the production line.

Process Cycle Efficiency: Process Cycle Efficiency (PCE) is a metric used in Lean to measure the effectiveness and efficiency of a process. It represents the ratio of value-added time to total cycle time, indicating the portion of the process time that adds value to the customer. A higher PCE indicates a more efficient and effective process, with less time wasted on non-value-adding activities. By measuring and improving PCE, organizations can identify areas of improvement and streamline their processes to deliver greater value to the customer.

Understanding and applying these terminologies is essential for managers seeking to implement Lean Six Sigma methodologies in their organizations. By embracing these concepts and incorporating them into daily operations, managers can drive a culture of continuous improvement, eliminate waste, and achieve operational excellence. **Lean is not just a set of tools and techniques; it is a mindset that fuels a relentless pursuit of perfection in all aspects of the business.**

SIX SIGMA BASICS

In today's rapidly changing business landscape, organizations are constantly striving to improve their processes and increase efficiency. Six Sigma has emerged from US-based company **Motorola**, as one of the most powerful methodologies to achieve these goals. As a Master Black Belt Certified Six Sigma practitioner, I have witnessed firsthand the transformative power of Six Sigma in various industries.

At its core, Six Sigma is focused on reducing variation and eliminating defects in a process. Variation refers to the differences or deviations from an ideal or target value. Defects, on the other hand, are any non-conformance with customer requirements. By reducing variation and eliminating defects, organizations can improve their processes, products, and services, ultimately leading to higher customer satisfaction and increased profitability.

One of the fundamental concepts of Six Sigma is **process capability**. Process capability is the ability of a process to consistently produce output within specified limits. It is a measure of how well a process meets customer requirements and expectations. A process with high capability has minimal variation and produces very few defects.

To better understand the concept of process capability, let me provide you with a simple example. Consider a manufacturing process that produces screws with a target length of 10 centimeters. If the process has high capability, the length of the screws produced will be very close to the target value, with minimal variation. However, if the process has low capability, there will be significant variation in the length of the screws, leading to defects such as screws that are too short or too long.

Now, let's delve into one of the most essential tools in Six Sigma: **Y=F(X).** Y represents the output or the dependent variable, while X represents the inputs or independent variables. The relationship between Y and X can be expressed using a mathematical equation, where Y is a function of X. This tool plays a critical role in process improvement by helping us understand how changes in the inputs or independent variables affect the output or dependent variable.

Imagine a scenario where a process is producing defective products. By utilizing the Y=F(X) tool, we can identify the key input variables that are causing the defects. For example, if we are manufacturing electronic devices and the defect rate is high, we can analyze the relationship between the defect rate (Y) and variables such as temperature, humidity, or manufacturing time (X) to pinpoint the root cause of the problem.

By understanding the relationship between the input variables and the output or dependent variable, we can make informed changes to the process to improve the output. This could involve adjusting the levels of the input variables or making changes to the process design. Ultimately, the goal is to minimize variation and eliminate defects, leading to improved process capability.

Data-driven decision-making is a cornerstone of Six Sigma. In the age of big data, organizations have access to vast amounts of information. However, without proper analysis and interpretation, this data is of little value. Statistical tools play a crucial role in analyzing data and identifying patterns, trends, and relationships that can lead to process improvements.

Hypothesis testing is one of the statistical tools used in Six Sigma. It helps us determine if there is a significant difference between two groups or if a particular factor has a meaningful impact on the process. By formulating a hypothesis and conducting statistical tests, we can make data-driven decisions and validate our assumptions.

Another powerful statistical tool used in Six Sigma is **regression analysis**. Regression analysis helps us understand the relationship between an independent variable and a dependent variable. It enables us to predict the value of the dependent variable based on the values of the independent variables.

Regression analysis can be used to identify the critical factors that influence the process and guide decision-making.

Design of experiments (DOE) is another statistical tool that is frequently used in Six Sigma. DOE allows us to systematically change the values of multiple variables and observe the impact on the output. By efficiently exploring the different combinations of input variables, we can determine the optimal settings that result in the desired output. DOE helps organizations achieve process optimization and improve overall performance.

Customer Need Analysis (CNA) and **Quality Function Deployment (QFD)** are two tools that emphasize the importance of understanding customer requirements and translating them into measurable and actionable targets. CNA helps us identify critical customer needs and prioritize them based on their impact and importance. QFD then takes these customer needs and aligns them with the organization's processes, ensuring that the products or services meet customer expectations.

In conclusion, this subchapter has provided an introduction to the basics of Six Sigma. We have explored concepts such as variation, defects, and process capability. The Y=F(X) tool has been explained with simple examples, showcasing its significance in process improvement. Furthermore, the subchapter has highlighted the importance of data-driven decision-making and the role of statistical tools in identifying and solving process problems.

By adopting Six Sigma principles and utilizing the tools and techniques discussed, organizations can achieve remarkable improvements in their processes, products, and services. Lean Six Sigma for Managers provides a comprehensive guide to implementing Six Sigma methodologies and driving operational excellence across various domains.

OVERVIEW OF DMAIC METHODOLOGY

Phase 1: Define

The first phase of the DMAIC methodology is the Define phase, which sets the foundation for any improvement project. During this phase, the focus is on understanding the current state of the process and identifying the key problem or opportunity for improvement. The key objective of this phase is to clearly define the project scope, goals, and deliverables. As a manager leading a DMAIC project, it is essential to rally the team around a shared understanding of the project's purpose and desired outcomes.

To begin the Define phase, it is crucial to have a cross-functional team that includes representatives from various stakeholders involved in the process. This team will play a critical role in gathering information, identifying customer needs, and setting project goals. The team will work collaboratively to define the problem statement and develop a project charter that outlines the project's scope, goals, timeline, and expected financial impact.

As a manager, your responsibility during the Define phase is to guide the team in clarifying the project objectives, ensuring alignment with organizational goals, and obtaining the necessary resources and support for the project. You will also need to facilitate discussions and engage stakeholders to gain a comprehensive understanding of the process and identify potential improvement opportunities.

Phase 2: Measure

The second phase of the DMAIC methodology is the Measure phase, where the focus shifts towards collecting data to establish a baseline and quantify the problem. It involves the selection of appropriate measurements, data collection methods, and the creation of measurement plans. The Measure phase aims to provide an objective assessment of the current performance of the process and identify areas of improvement.

During this phase, your role as a manager is to guide the team in identifying the critical metrics that will be used to evaluate the performance of the process. You will help the team in establishing a robust data collection plan, ensuring that the data collected is accurate, reliable, and representative of the process. You will also support the team in identifying potential sources of data and guide them in selecting appropriate measurement techniques.

As the leader of a DMAIC project, you must emphasize the importance of data integrity and ensure that the team is using reliable statistical tools and techniques to analyze the data. This phase requires a meticulous approach to data collection and measurement system analysis to ensure that the data accurately reflects the process's performance.

Phase 3: Analyze

The third phase of the DMAIC methodology is the Analyze phase, where the focus is on understanding the root causes of the problem identified in the Define phase. The analysis phase involves using data-driven tools and techniques to identify the factors that contribute most significantly to the problem and to prioritize improvement opportunities.

During the Analyze phase, your role as a manager is to guide the team in applying various statistical and analytical tools to investigate the data collected during the Measure phase. You will help the team identify potential causes of the problem using tools such as regression analysis, hypothesis testing, and design of experiments. Your expertise in data analysis and statistical techniques will be crucial in guiding the team towards the identification of root causes.

Furthermore, you will need to guide the team in establishing cause-and-effect relationships and determining the critical X (input variables) that have the most significant impact on the Y (output variable). This phase requires a comprehensive analysis of the process data to ensure that the team has a clear understanding of the drivers of the problem.

Phase 4: Improve

The fourth phase of the DMAIC methodology is the Improve phase, where the focus shifts towards generating and implementing solutions to address the root causes identified in the Analyze phase. This phase involves brainstorming, evaluating potential solutions, and piloting innovative changes to the process.

As a manager, your role during the Improve phase is to foster a culture of creativity and innovation within the team. You will facilitate brainstorming sessions, guide the team in generating potential solutions, and provide guidance in evaluating and selecting the most feasible and impactful solutions. Moreover, you will need to support the team in developing an implementation plan and conducting pilot tests to validate the effectiveness of the proposed improvements.

In addition to your role as a facilitator, you will also be responsible for ensuring that the improvements align with the organization's strategic goals and that they can be implemented within the allocated resources and timeline. Your expertise in lean and Six Sigma tools will be invaluable in guiding the team toward sustainable improvements that drive meaningful change within the process.

Phase 5: Control

The final phase of the DMAIC methodology is the Control phase, where the focus is on ensuring that the improvements made during the improve phase are sustained over time. The Control phase involves implementing control mechanisms, creating monitoring plans, and developing standard operating procedures to ensure ongoing process stability and performance.

As a project lead, your role during the Control phase is to guide the team in developing control plans that outline the measures and tools required to maintain the improved state of the process. You will help in establishing process controls, developing monitoring systems, and implementing mechanisms to prevent the recurrence of the problem. Your expertise in quality function deployment and statistical process control will be essential in ensuring that the process remains stable and in control.

Moreover, you will need to create a culture of accountability and continuous improvement within the team. This includes developing training programs, conducting regular audits, and establishing feedback mechanisms to monitor the performance of the process and address any deviations. The Control phase requires a sustained effort to ensure that the improvements made during the DMAIC project are embedded within the organization's operations and become part of the standard way of working.

In conclusion, the DMAIC methodology provides a structured approach to process improvement, enabling managers to lead teams effectively through each phase of the improvement journey. As a manager, your role is critical in guiding the team, providing expertise, and ensuring the successful execution of the DMAIC project. By following this methodology and embracing a data-driven and systematic approach, organizations can achieve significant and sustainable process improvements that drive operational excellence.

ROLES AND RESPONSIBILITIES OF SIX SIGMA BELTS

1. Project Sponsor:

The Project Sponsor plays a crucial role in ensuring the success of a DMAIC project. They are typically high-level executives who have the authority and resources to support the project. The Project Sponsor provides clear objectives, aligns the project with overall business goals, and ensures that adequate resources are allocated. They also remove any obstacles or roadblocks that may hinder the progress of the project. The Project Sponsor is responsible for championing the project, securing executive buy-in, and communicating the project's progress to the senior management team.

2. Project Champion:

The Project Champion is typically a mid-level manager who directly supports and advocates for the DMAIC project. They work closely with the Black Belt to ensure that the project aligns with the organization's strategic objectives and remains on track. The Project Champion provides guidance, facilitates communication between team members, and helps to remove any obstacles that may impede progress. They also serve as a liaison between the project team and the senior management team, communicating the project's impact and benefits to the organization.

3. Master Black Belt:

As a Master Black Belt, I have the privilege of leading and mentoring other Six Sigma practitioners, including Black Belts, Green Belts, and Yellow Belts. My responsibilities include providing guidance on the methodology, reviewing and monitoring the progress of DMAIC projects, and ensuring adherence to the Six Sigma principles and standards. Additionally, I conduct training sessions and workshops to enhance the skills and knowledge of the Six Sigma team members. I am also responsible for identifying areas of improvement within the organization and leading projects to address these areas.

4. Black Belt:

The Black Belt is a highly trained and experienced Six Sigma professional who leads DMAIC projects. Their role is to apply the Six Sigma methodology, tools, and techniques to identify, analyze, and improve processes within the organization. They are responsible for managing the project from start to finish, including defining the project scope, creating a project plan, leading the project team, and monitoring progress. Black Belts work closely with the Project Champion and the Master Black Belt to ensure the successful completion of the project.

5. Green Belt:

The Green Belt is a Six Sigma practitioner who works on DMAIC projects under the guidance of a Black Belt. Green Belts are usually individuals who have undergone training and have a good understanding of the Six Sigma methodology. They contribute to the project by collecting and analyzing data, identifying improvement opportunities, and implementing solutions. Green Belts may also lead smaller-scale projects or assist the Black Belt in larger projects. Their role is critical in supporting the Black Belt and ensuring the successful implementation of process improvements.

6. Yellow Belt:

The Yellow Belt is an entry-level Six Sigma practitioner who supports the DMAIC projects. They are responsible for assisting the Black Belt and the Green Belt in data collection, analysis, and process documentation. Yellow Belts may also participate in improvement activities and contribute to problem-solving initiatives within their respective areas. While their role may be less extensive than other belts, Yellow Belts play a valuable supporting role in the successful execution of Six Sigma projects.

7. White Belt:

The White Belt is the introductory level of Six Sigma certification. White Belts have a basic understanding of the Six Sigma philosophy and principles but do not actively participate in DMAIC projects. They may be individuals who are interested in learning about Six Sigma or have a peripheral involvement with the projects. While not directly involved in project work, White Belts may provide support by participating in training workshops or brainstorming sessions.

In summary, the success of a DMAIC project heavily depends on the roles and responsibilities of the Six Sigma belts involved. From the Project Sponsor and Project Champion, who set the project's direction, to the Master Black Belt, Black Belt, Green Belt, Yellow Belt, and even the White Belt, each role contributes to the overall success of the project. The effective collaboration and coordination between these roles ensure the implementation of sustainable process improvements, leading to increased efficiency, reduced defects, and improved customer satisfaction. By understanding and fulfilling their respective responsibilities, the Six Sigma team can drive impactful change within organizations and foster a culture of continuous improvement.

CHAPTER 2: DEFINE PHASE

OVERVIEW OF DEFINE PHASE

In this subchapter, I will provide an in-depth overview of the define phase, focusing on the three essential steps: problem identification, project selection, and project charter preparation. I will also recommend the appropriate Six Sigma tools to be used at each step, ensuring that the final deliverable is an approved project charter.

Problem Identification:

The first step in the define phase is to identify the problem. This involves thoroughly understanding the current state of affairs, gathering relevant data, and recognizing the gap between the existing situation and the desired performance. This step requires a systematic approach to ensure that the problem is accurately defined and prioritized. As the saying goes, "A problem well-defined is half-done."

To effectively identify the problem, several tools and techniques can be employed. The important tools for problem identification are Voice of Customer, Voice of Business, Cost of Poor Quality, and Brainstorming. Another useful tool is SIPOC (Supplier, Input, Process, Output, Customer), which provides a high-level overview of the process and helps identify potential areas of improvement.

Project Selection:

Once the problem has been identified, the next step is to select the appropriate project. This involves evaluating the potential projects based on their alignment with the organization's strategic goals, available resources, and expected impact on business outcomes. Project selection is a critical step in ensuring that the limited resources are effectively utilized to target the most significant areas of improvement.

To facilitate project selection, a variety of tools and techniques can be employed. For instance, the Pugh matrix is a systematic decision-making tool that helps evaluate and compare multiple project options based on predefined criteria. It allows for an objective assessment of the projects and aids in selecting the most viable option. Other techniques, such as multi-voting and impact effort matrix, can also be used to facilitate the decision-making process and prioritize projects based on their potential benefits.

Project Charter Preparation:

The final step in the define phase is the preparation of a project charter. The project charter serves as a roadmap for the entire project, outlining its objectives, scope, timeline, and expected deliverables. It plays a crucial role in aligning the project with the organization's strategic goals and securing stakeholders' commitment.

The project charter should clearly define the problem statement, including the nature and magnitude of the problem, as well as its impact on business outcomes. Additionally, it should outline the project's objectives, specifying what the project aims to achieve and how it will be measured. The project team should be identified, and their roles and responsibilities should be clearly defined. It is also essential to determine the project's scope, set boundaries, and identify which processes and areas will be included or excluded.

Tools such as the Gantt chart and critical path method (CPM) can be utilized to assist in the development of a project timeline and to identify critical project milestones. These tools help ensure that the project remains on track and that the team is aware of key checkpoints. Furthermore, a stakeholder analysis can be conducted to identify and engage key stakeholders, ensuring their support throughout the project.

The define phase is a critical part of the DMAIC methodology and sets the stage for the entire project. By accurately identifying the problem, selecting the right project, and preparing a comprehensive project charter, organizations can ensure that the project is aligned with their strategic goals and has a higher chance of success.

In conclusion, the three important steps of the define phase, namely problem identification, project selection, and project charter preparation, play a crucial role in the success of a DMAIC project. By employing the appropriate Six Sigma tools at each step, organizations can effectively identify and prioritize problems, select the most viable projects, and develop thorough project charters. The define phase ensures that the project is aligned with the organization's goals and that stakeholders are committed to its success. It forms the foundation for the subsequent steps in the DMAIC methodology and sets the project on the path to achieving its desired outcomes.

Major Steps	• Step 1: Generate Project Ideas
	• Step 2: Select Project
	• Step 3: Finalize Project Charter & High-Level Process Map
Important questions to be answered	• Is your project important to business? • Has the chosen project been aligned with organization goals? • Does a business case exist in the chosen project? • Is your project goal measurable and achievable? • Have you identified the customers and their requirements? • Are project plan and key milestones defined?
Main deliverables	• Approved Project Charter • High Level Process Map

PROBLEM IDENTIFICATION

To begin, let us discuss the power of Brainstorming. This creative problem-solving technique allows teams to generate a large number of ideas and potential improvement opportunities. By encouraging open and uninhibited discussion, Brainstorming harnesses the collective knowledge and expertise of team members. It is important for organizations to create an environment that encourages participation and ensures that all ideas are given equal consideration. In my experience, a diverse group of stakeholders, representing different functions and levels within the organization, can contribute significantly during the Brainstorming process. As a facilitator, my role is to guide the session, foster collaboration, and capture all ideas for further evaluation.

Once the ideas have been brainstormed, it is crucial to prioritize them based on their impact and feasibility. This is where the **Voice of the Customer (VOC) Analysis** becomes instrumental. VOC analysis involves capturing and analyzing customer feedback and requirements to identify areas for improvement. By understanding the needs and expectations of our customers, we can focus our efforts on activities that will bring the most value. VOC analysis can be conducted through surveys, interviews, and other feedback mechanisms. It is essential to involve representatives from the customer-facing functions, as their insights are invaluable in understanding the pain points and identifying opportunities for improvement.

While the Voice of the Customer is critical, we must also consider the **Voice of the Business (VOB)**. VOB analysis helps us align our improvement efforts with key business objectives. It involves engaging with senior leaders and decision-makers to understand their vision, strategic priorities, and pain points. By bringing together the perspectives of both the customer and the organization, we can identify improvement opportunities that not only enhance customer satisfaction but also drive business growth and profitability. VOB analysis enables us to prioritize improvement projects based on their relevance to the organization's overall goals.

In addition to VOC and VOB analysis, another tool that aids in problem identification is the **Cost of Poor Quality (COPQ) analysis**. COPQ analysis quantifies the financial impact of poor quality, including both internal and external costs. Internally, poor quality can result in rework, waste, and lower productivity. Externally, the cost of poor quality can manifest as customer complaints, warranty claims, and lost business opportunities. By conducting a thorough COPQ analysis, we can identify processes and areas with the highest impact and prioritize improvement efforts accordingly. COPQ analysis serves as a compelling argument for investing in continuous improvement initiatives by showcasing the potential financial benefits they can deliver.

The success of problem identification heavily relies on the involvement and engagement of key stakeholders. It is vital to include individuals from different departments and functions who have a vested interest in the outcomes of process improvement initiatives. In my experience, involving stakeholders from different levels within the organization brings diverse perspectives and ensures that the identified problems are representative of the overall business needs. Stakeholder involvement also fosters a sense of ownership and responsibility, making them more likely to support the improvement initiatives.

Furthermore, aligning project goals with organizational objectives is paramount to ensure that process improvement efforts are focused and meaningful. The identified problem areas should directly contribute to the organization's overall strategy and desired outcomes. By clearly articulating the project goals and linking them to the strategic priorities, we create a sense of purpose and direction for the improvement initiatives. This alignment also helps in garnering support and resources from senior leadership, who are instrumental in driving change across the organization.

To illustrate the concepts discussed so far, let us consider a hypothetical example in the manufacturing industry. A company that produces electronic devices has been experiencing a high rate of product returns due to non-functional components. The problem identification process would begin by assembling a cross-functional team, consisting of representatives from manufacturing, quality assurance, design, and customer service departments. During the Brainstorming session, team members would generate ideas such as improving manufacturing processes, enhancing component testing protocols, and enhancing supplier quality management practices.

The VOC analysis would involve surveying the customers who faced issues with the non-functional components. The feedback received would shed light on the specific aspects of the product that failed to meet their expectations. Simultaneously, the VOB analysis would involve discussions with senior leaders to understand the company's strategic priorities and financial goals. This analysis would help identify specific areas of focus, such as reducing warranty claims and improving customer satisfaction, that align with the organization's objectives.

Following this, a COPQ analysis could be conducted by quantifying the financial impact of product returns, warranty claims, and customer complaints. This analysis would help prioritize improvement efforts by highlighting the processes and areas that have the highest cost of poor quality.

Throughout the problem identification process, key stakeholders, including senior leaders, manufacturing supervisors, and quality assurance engineers, would be actively involved. Their diverse perspectives and expertise would contribute to comprehensive problem identification. By involving various stakeholders and aligning project goals with organizational objectives, the problem-identification process ensures that improvement initiatives are purposeful and effective. It sets the foundation for implementing Lean and Six Sigma methodologies, DMAIC tools, and techniques, thereby positioning the organization on a path of continuous improvement and operational excellence. In the next subchapter, we will explore in detail the Lean and Six Sigma tools and techniques that aid in problem-solving and process improvement.

ACTIVITY – 1: VOC TO CTQ

VOC is the expression of the customer's needs and expectations, while critical to quality (CTQ) is the measurable attribute that meets those needs. To identify CTQs from VOC, you can use a tool known as CTQ tree. A CTQ tree is a diagram that shows the hierarchy of customer needs, drivers and CTQs. For example, if the customer need is to have a fast and reliable internet connection, the driver could be the speed and stability of the service, and the CTQ could be the bandwidth and latency of the network.

Converting the VOC into CTQ parameters is a crucial step in the Six Sigma methodology. It involves translating customer needs and requirements into specific, measurable, and actionable metrics to guide the improvement of processes. Let's walk through an example to illustrate this process:

Step 1: Detect Voice of the Customer

Voice of the Customer Statement: "I want a durable and comfortable backpack for hiking trips."

Step 2: Identify the customer needs

It highlights the customer requirements and it is the origin of a CTQ tree.

Need-1: The customer wants the backpack to withstand the rigors of hiking and outdoor activities.

Need-2: The customer desires a backpack that is comfortable to carry for extended periods.

Step 3: Identify the drivers of satisfaction

Drivers are the parameters on which a customer judges the quality of product.

Driver-1: Durability; Driver-2: Comfortable

Step 4: Convert the drivers to Critical-to-Quality (CTQ) Characteristics

CTQs are the measurable characteristics that have to be met to satisfy clients. It helps the quality teams to measure quality of a product and service and make sure it meets client's demands.

CTQ Parameter for Durability: **"Backpack Material Strength"**

Metric: Tensile Strength (measured in pounds per square inch, psi)

Target: Tensile strength of at least 1000 psi is required to ensure durability

CTQ Parameter for Comfortableness: **"Backpack Weight Distribution"**

Metric: Evenness of weight distribution (measured as a percentage)

Target: Weight should be distributed evenly across the backpack to minimize discomfort during extended use

These CTQ parameters are specific and measurable, and provide actionable guidance for the design and manufacturing processes. The team responsible for creating or improving the backpack can now focus on meeting these CTQ targets to ensure that the final product aligns with the customer's needs.

In this example, the customer's desire for a durable and comfortable backpack has been translated into two CTQ parameters: "Backpack Material Strength" and "Backpack Weight Distribution." These CTQ parameters will guide the design, manufacturing, and testing processes to ensure that the final product meets the customer's expectations.

We want to inform you that the CTQ parameters may vary based on the industry, product, or service being considered. The goal is to capture the essence of what the customer values and translate it into measurable parameters that can be used to drive process improvements and ensure customer satisfaction.

In summary, the Voice of the Customer is a crucial aspect of customer-centric organizations, as it provides valuable insights that help businesses understand and meet customer expectations, improve customer satisfaction, and drive business growth.

Additional Examples & DIY Exercise:

VOC Statement	Drivers	CTQ Metric
1. **Call Centre:** "It would be great if the customer support team could provide faster response times and more personalized assistance."	Time	Response time
2. **Sales and Marketing:** "I value competitive pricing and would appreciate more affordable options for your products."	Price	Product Price
3. **Software development:** "The website navigation is confusing, and I often struggle to find the information I need."	Easy to use	No. of clicks to find a specific information from homepage
4. **E-Commerce:** "The checkout process is too complicated, and it discourages me from completing my purchase."	Fast	Checkout Process Time
5. **Sales and Marketing:** "I would love to see more variety in product options to better cater to different customer preferences and needs."	Multiple options	Number of variants
6. **Automotive Industry:** "I want a car with advanced safety features that provide a secure driving experience for my family."	No. of safety features	Air Bags, Adaptive cruise control, Lane assist, Blind spot information system,
7. **Electronics Industry:** " I love the high-resolution camera on my phone, but I wish the battery life was longer. I find myself needing to charge it multiple times a day, which is inconvenient."	Camera Resolution Battery Capacity Backup Hours	Mega Pixel level Battery mAH level 8 Hours
8. **Home Appliances Industry:** "I want a washing machine with a larger capacity and energy-efficient features to reduce water and electricity consumption."	Capacity Power Consumption	8 litres Star rating

DO IT YOURSELF EXERCISE		
9. **Food and Beverage Industry:** "I expect the food packaging to be leak-proof and easily resealable for convenience and freshness"		
10. **Healthcare Industry:** "I can't wait too long to see a doctorand I need a personalized care"		
11. **Construction Industry:** " We need high-quality construction and timely delivery"		
12. **Personal Care Industry:** "I prefer skincare products that show visible results"		
13. **Aerospace Industry:** "I expect aircraft components to be lightweight without compromising on safety and durability."		
14. **Energy Industry:** "I want renewable energy solutions that can help reduce my carbon footprint and contribute to a greener environment."		
15. **Clothing and Fashion Industry:** "I prefer clothing made from sustainable and organic materials for ethical and environmental reasons."		
Write few example cases from your workplace		
16.		
17.		
18.		
19.		
20.		

ACTIVITY – 2: VOB TO CTB

VOB in Six Sigma projects is a summary of the needs, goals and pain points of the business and its stakeholders, such as profitability, revenue, growth, and market share1. It helps to align the project with the strategic objectives of the organization and to balance the other voices, such as the voice of the customer (VoC), the voice of the process (VoP), the voice of the employees (VoE), and the voice of the data (VoD)

Critical to business (CTB) characteristics in Six Sigma are the key factors that determine the success of the business and its alignment with the strategic objectives of the organization. Some examples of CTB characteristics are: Profitability, Revenue, Growth, Market share, Customer satisfaction, Process efficiency, Quality, Innovation.

Here are a few examples of Voice of the Business (VoB) statements within the context of Six Sigma:

1. "Our business objective is to reduce production costs by 10% within the next fiscal year while maintaining product quality standards." – **Production Cost**

2. "We need to improve our order fulfilment process to reduce lead time and increase customer satisfaction." – **Order fulfilment lead time, CSAT Score**

VOB, when converted to CTB provide a clear direction for improvement initiatives within the framework of Six Sigma, helping to prioritize projects and allocate resources effectively.

Additional Examples & DIY Exercise:

VOB Statement	CTB Metric
1. "Increasing customer retention is a top priority for our business. We need to identify and address the root causes of customer churn."	Churn rate (%)
2. "Our goal is to improve operational efficiency by reducing waste and optimizing resource utilization."	OEE (%)
3. "We want to enhance product reliability and reduce the number of product returns and warranty claims."	Product returns / month Warranty claim (Lakhs)
DO IT YOURSELF EXERCISE	
4. "Minimizing defects and errors in our manufacturing process is critical to ensure consistent product quality and customer satisfaction."	
5. "We need to streamline our supply chain to improve delivery reliability and reduce inventory holding costs."	
6. "We are committed to improving customer service response time and resolving customer issues more effectively."	
7. "We need to optimize our customer acquisition process to increase market share and expand our customer base."	

8. "Improving the efficiency of our manufacturing operations is key to meeting increasing demand and maintaining profitability."	
9. "Reducing product defects and rework is essential to minimize costs and enhance customer satisfaction."	
10. "Enhancing our supplier management process is critical for ensuring timely delivery of high-quality materials and components."	
Write few example cases from your workplace	
11.	
12.	
13.	
14.	
15.	

ACTIVITY – 3: COPQ & COGQ

The Cost of Poor Quality (COPQ) refers to the financial impact of producing defective products or delivering poor-quality services. It encompasses both the tangible and intangible costs associated with poor quality. Here are some components of the Cost of Poor Quality:

1. Internal Failure Costs: These costs are incurred when defects are identified before products or services reach the customer. Examples include rework, scrap, repair, and downtime.

2. External Failure Costs: These costs occur when defective products or services reach the customer and are identified externally. They can include warranty claims, returns, customer complaints, product recalls, and legal actions.

It is important to note that the actual cost of poor quality can vary significantly depending on the industry, company size, and specific circumstances. However, studies have consistently shown that poor quality can be a significant financial burden for organizations, ranging from 15% to 30% or more of their total revenue.

The Cost of Good Quality (COGQ) refers to the expenses incurred to ensure and maintain high-quality products or services. It includes the costs associated with prevention and appraisal activities aimed at preventing defects and ensuring that quality standards are met. Here are some components of the Cost of Good Quality:

1. Prevention Costs: These are the expenses incurred to prevent quality issues from occurring. They include activities such as quality planning, training programs, process documentation, supplier evaluations, and implementing quality management systems.

2. Appraisal Costs: These are the costs incurred to assess and verify the quality of products or services. They include activities like inspections, testing, quality audits, equipment calibration, and quality control measures.

Investing in prevention and appraisal activities helps organizations identify and address potential quality issues early in the process, improving product reliability, customer satisfaction, and overall quality performance. The goal is to achieve a balance between prevention and appraisal costs to maximize quality while minimizing overall costs. Cost of Good Quality and Cost of Poor Quality together Is known as Cost of Quality.

Additional Examples & DIY Exercise:

COQ Element	Prevention / Appraisal / Internal / External Failure
1. Calibration of measuring equipment: Costs incurred to calibrate measuring equipment used in quality control.	Appraisal Cost
2. Customer complaint: Costs incurred in handling customer complaints, returns, and warranty claims.	External Failure Cost
3. Downtime and disruption: Costs resulting from production interruptions caused by quality issues.	Internal Failure Cost
4. Equipment maintenance: Costs involved in maintaining equipment to prevent quality issues.	Prevention Cost
DO IT YOURSELF EXERCISE	
5. Field service and repairs: Costs associated with providing service or repairs to products that fail in the field.	

6. Inspection and testing: Costs associated with inspecting and testing products to ensure they meet quality standards.	
7. Internal quality failure analysis: Costs involved in investigating the causes of internal quality failures and corrective actions.	
8. Process documentation: Costs involved in documenting procedures, work instructions, and quality control plans.	
9. Product recalls: Costs involved in recalling and replacing products due to safety or quality concerns.	
10. Quality planning and design: Costs associated with activities aimed at ensuring that products or services meet specifications during the planning and design phase.	
11. Scrap and rework: Costs incurred due to the rejection of products or services and the need for rework or repair.	
12. Supplier evaluation and audits: Costs associated with assessing and monitoring the quality of suppliers' products.	
13. Training: Costs incurred to train employees on quality standards, processes, and techniques.	
14. Warranty claims and litigation: Costs resulting from warranty claims, lawsuits, and legal settlements.	
Write few example cases from your workplace	
15.	
16.	
17.	
18.	
19.	
20.	

PARETO ANALYSIS FOR PROBLEM STRATIFICATION

Picture yourself in a jam, my friend. You've got a laundry list of problems staring you in the face, and it feels like an uphill battle to tackle each one. You're drowning in a sea of issues, without a clue which ones are truly important and which ones are just there to annoy you. But fear not, because Pareto analysis is here to save the day. It's like a superhero that swoops in, helping managers and leaders figure out which problems deserve their immediate attention, while pushing the pesky ones aside.

Let me paint you a picture with a real-life example from the garment industry. There was this clothing manufacturer that was drowning in customer complaints and rejections. They were desperate to uncover the root causes behind these issues, but they realized that they needed to prioritize their efforts. So they turned to Pareto analysis, hoping it would shed some light on the matter.

The first step in the Pareto analysis dance is to gather all the data on the problems at hand. In this case, our clothing heroes collected information on customer complaints and rejection reasons over a specific period. They sorted these issues into categories like defective buttons, stitching defects, loose threads, color fading, and cloth tear. Armed with this data, they were ready to dive into the analysis.

Using Pareto analysis is like taking a wild roller coaster ride. You plot the frequency of each problem category on a graph, from most to least frequent. This graph, also known as a Pareto chart, visually shows you the impact of each problem category, like a colorful explosion of information.

When the analysis was finally complete, it was as if a light bulb had gone off in the room. Only a few categories were causing the majority of the customer complaints. Defective buttons, stitching defects, and loose threads were the troublemakers, the major issues that needed immediate attention.

With this newfound knowledge, our heroes were able to shift their focus and resources to these vital few issues. No more chasing ghosts or getting tangled up in trivial problems. It was time to dig deeper and really understand what was causing these issues.

As they peeled back the layers of the problem, they made an incredible discovery. Most of the defective buttons were coming from the shirts section. This was a breakthrough moment, my friend. They realized that the button misalignment in the shirts section was causing all the trouble. Customers were complaining and rejecting shirts left and right.

This level of precision in problem identification would not have been possible without Pareto analysis. It didn't just help them separate the important from the trivial, it also laid out a roadmap for further investigation and improvement.

Armed with this newfound clarity, our heroes embarked on a quest to find solutions for the button misalignment issue. They pulled out all the stops, using their expertise in Lean and Six Sigma methodologies. They whipped out their trusty toolbox, with tools like DMAIC (Define, Measure, Analyze, Improve, Control) and Statistical Process Control.

Through their investigation, they unraveled a web of factors contributing to button misalignment. It was like untangling a mess of threads. They found that machine calibration, operator skill and training, and material quality were all playing a part in this button catastrophe. They dug deep, analyzing the root causes, brainstorming ideas, and testing out different solutions.

Finally, they hit the jackpot. They implemented targeted improvements, like training the operators, recalibrating the machines, and sourcing higher-quality buttons. They kept a watchful eye on the process, monitoring and measuring to make sure the changes were making a real difference.

And boy, did it pay off! By tackling the button misalignment problem head-on, they saw a massive reduction in customer complaints and rejections. The product quality improved, customers were happier, and the company's reputation soared to new heights.

This little tale shows you the power of Pareto analysis in action. Without it, the company would have wasted precious time and resources chasing after less impactful issues. But thanks to this analysis tool, they were able to cut through the noise and focus on the problems that would make the biggest difference.

In a nutshell, Pareto analysis is a lifesaver for managers and leaders. It helps them prioritize their time and resources, guiding them towards the vital few problems that need immediate attention. By narrowing down and scoping the problem effectively, organizations can make the most of their resources and achieve remarkable improvements.

ACTIVITY – 4: PARETO ANALYSIS

Post a recent promotional campaign, HFCD bank's monthly debit card applications increased from 4500 to 8000. They would usually have 11% incomplete applications however now the % increased to 19%. The process manager listed down all the sections in the form and frequency of each section not been completed. Please carry out appropriate analysis to identify the vital few sections which when fixed will reduce % incomplete applications. Also, fill-up the table below. (Refer excel file for data: DC_Application.mtw)

Total No. of sections in the application form	
No. of sections contributing to 80% of errors	
No. of sections contributing to the remaining errors	

Sections	Frequency
Name as they want to be on the card	1
Nationality	1
Date of Birth	241
No. of dependents	2
Pan number	12
ID card number	11
Present address	1
Present address Type	24
Landmark near residence	59
Email address	2
Landline number	146
Tenure of Stay at Present Address	1
Preferred contact time	4
Mailing address: Residence/ Office	14
Work related details	169
Income details	179
Spouse details	69
References contact details	84
Other Bank CC details	169
Existing relationship with the bank	14
Account details of the bank	2
Staying Informed	102
Registration-free services	112

PROJECT CHARTER

The project charter is a document that outlines the business case, problem statement, goal statement, scope statement, team members, and timeline of the DMAIC project. It serves as a communication tool for all stakeholders involved, ensuring that everyone is aligned and working towards a common goal. Developing a project charter requires a systematic approach in order to capture all the necessary information and set the project up for success.

Step 1: Understanding the Problem

The first step in developing a project charter is to clearly define the problem at hand. This involves gathering data, conducting interviews, and speaking with subject matter experts. As a manager, it is important to take the time to truly understand the problem before moving forward. This step may involve analyzing historical data, conducting process walks, and engaging with team members to gain insights into the current state of affairs. By understanding the problem in depth, managers can uncover the root causes and identify potential improvement opportunities.

Step 2: Establishing the Business Case

Once the problem has been clearly defined, the next step is to establish the business case for the project. The business case outlines the justification for undertaking the project, including the potential benefits, return on investment, and alignment with organizational objectives. It is important for managers to clearly articulate the reasons why this project is important for the organization and how it will contribute to the overall success. This step involves conducting a cost-benefit analysis and weighing the potential risks and rewards of the project.

Step 3: Defining the Goal Statement

The goal statement is a succinct and measurable statement that identifies the specific objectives of the project. It outlines what the project aims to achieve and how success will be measured. As a manager, it is important to create a goal statement that is specific, measurable, attainable, relevant, and time-bound (SMART). This step involves aligning the project goals with the organizational goals and ensuring that they are realistic and achievable.

Step 4: Establishing the Scope Statement

The scope statement defines the boundaries of the project and outlines what will be included and excluded. It helps to set realistic expectations and ensures that the project remains focused. As a manager, it is important to clearly define the scope of the project, taking into consideration any constraints or limitations. This step may involve conducting a stakeholder analysis and understanding the expectations and requirements of all parties involved.

Step 5: Identifying the Team Members

A DMAIC project requires a multidisciplinary team with diverse skills and expertise. In this step, it is important for managers to identify the key team members who will be responsible for driving the project forward. This may include subject matter experts, process owners, data analysts, and other stakeholders. It is crucial to select team members who are committed, knowledgeable, and willing to contribute their time and expertise to the project. In addition, it is important to define the roles and responsibilities of each team member to ensure clarity and accountability.

Step 6: Establishing the Timeline

The timeline of the project is an essential component of the project charter. It provides a roadmap for the team members and helps to ensure that the project stays on track. As a manager, it is important to establish a realistic and achievable timeline, taking into consideration any competing priorities or resource limitations. This step involves creating a project schedule, identifying key milestones, and establishing deadlines for each phase of the DMAIC process. It is important to regularly monitor and update the timeline as the project progresses to ensure that deadlines are met and the project remains on schedule.

Benefits of a Well-Defined Project Charter

Having a well-defined project charter is critical for ensuring the success of any DMAIC project. The project charter serves as a communication tool, aligning all stakeholders and providing a clear roadmap for the team members to follow. Some of the key benefits of a well-defined project charter include:

1. Clear Direction: The project charter clarifies the goals, objectives, and scope of the project, ensuring that everyone is moving in the same direction. This helps to prevent confusion and keeps the project focused on the desired outcome.

2. Stakeholder Alignment: By involving all stakeholders in the development of the project charter, managers can ensure that everyone is aligned and working towards a common goal. This minimizes resistance to change and increases the likelihood of project success.

3. Improved Decision-Making: The project charter provides a framework for decision-making throughout the project. It helps to prioritize tasks, allocate resources, and make informed decisions based on data and facts.

4. Increased Accountability: By clearly defining roles and responsibilities in the project charter, managers can hold team members accountable for their contributions. This helps to promote a culture of ownership and ensures that everyone is actively engaged in the project.

5. Risk Mitigation: The project charter helps to identify potential risks and develop appropriate mitigation strategies. By addressing risks early on, managers can minimize the likelihood of project delays or failures.

In conclusion, the project charter is a vital component of any DMAIC project. It provides the foundation for the project, ensuring that all stakeholders are aligned and working towards a common goal. By following a systematic approach to developing a comprehensive project charter, managers can set their projects up for success. This subchapter has provided a step-by-step process for understanding the problem and creating a project charter. It has also highlighted the benefits of having a well-defined project charter in ensuring project success. As a Master Black Belt Certified Six Sigma Practitioner, I have seen the power of a well-executed project charter in driving organizational improvement. I encourage managers to utilize the insights and guidance provided in this subchapter to develop their own project charters and embark on their improvement journey with confidence.

SIPOC

The SIPOC tool serves as a visual representation of the process, providing clarity on the sequence of activities, the parties involved, and the key deliverables at each stage. It serves as a foundation for further analysis and improvement efforts, allowing managers to identify potential areas of improvement and make informed decisions.

Let's start by understanding each component of the SIPOC framework in more detail.

1. Suppliers: Suppliers are entities or individuals who provide inputs to the process. They could be internal or external to the organization. These inputs can take various forms, such as raw materials, information, or services. Suppliers play a critical role in ensuring the availability and quality of inputs, which directly impact the process outcomes. For example, in a manufacturing process, suppliers could be material vendors, while in a customer service process, suppliers could be internal teams or external partner organizations.

2. Inputs: Inputs are the materials, data, or resources that flow into the process. They are the raw materials or triggers that initiate the process. Understanding the inputs is crucial as it helps identify the sources of variation and potential bottlenecks. Inputs could include physical materials, documents, customer requests, or even verbal instructions. For instance, in a procurement process, inputs could be purchase requisitions, specifications, or material requirements. In a software development process, inputs could be user stories, design documents, or customer feedback.

3. Processes: The process component of the SIPOC framework describes the series of steps or activities required to transform inputs into outputs. These activities can be both manual and automated, and they need to be executed in a specific sequence to achieve the desired outcomes. The process includes not only the core value-adding activities but also any support processes required to enable smooth operations. Understanding the process flow is essential for identifying potential bottlenecks, waste, or non-value-added activities. It also helps identify opportunities for automation or streamlining the process. For instance, in a manufacturing process, the activities could involve material preparation, assembly, inspection, and packaging. In a sales process, the activities could include lead generation, qualification, presentation, negotiation, and closing.

4. Outputs: Outputs are the final products, services, or deliverables produced by the process. They represent the value that the process delivers to the customers or stakeholders. Outputs can be tangible or intangible, and they can take various forms such as physical goods, reports, invoices, or customer satisfaction metrics. Understanding the outputs is crucial for determining whether the process is meeting the intended goals and objectives. It also helps identify any gaps or deviations from customer requirements. For example, in a manufacturing process, outputs could be finished goods ready for shipment. In a customer support process, outputs could be resolved issues, customer satisfaction ratings, or service level agreements.

5. Customers: Customers are the recipients or beneficiaries of the process outputs. They could be internal or external to the organization. Understanding who the customers are and their specific needs is critical for aligning the process with customer requirements. It helps identify gaps or areas of improvement to enhance customer satisfaction. Customers can be individuals, departments, or external entities such as suppliers or end-users. For example, in a manufacturing process, the customers could be wholesalers or retailers who purchase the finished goods. In a healthcare process, the customers could be patients, medical professionals, or insurance companies.

Now that we have a clear understanding of each component of SIPOC, let's explore how it can be applied in practice. To illustrate its application, let's consider an example of a software development process.

Suppliers: The suppliers in this case could be the product management team, who provide requirements and specifications for the software. They could also include external vendors who provide software tools or platforms.

Inputs: The inputs to the software development process could include user stories, design documents, technical specifications, and customer feedback. These inputs serve as the foundation for the development activities.

Processes: The process would involve various activities such as requirement analysis, design, coding, testing, and deployment. It could also include support processes such as version control, bug tracking, and documentation.

Outputs: The outputs of the process would be functional software applications that meet the customer's requirements. These could be tangible deliverables such as the software package or intangible deliverables such as error-free code or user-friendly interfaces.

Customers: The customers in this case could be end-users who will be using the software, as well as other stakeholders such as the product management team, quality assurance team, or sales team.

By mapping out the SIPOC for this software development process, managers gain a holistic view of the process. They can identify potential areas of improvement, such as optimizing the requirement-gathering process or streamlining the testing activities. They can also identify key stakeholders and their specific needs, enabling better alignment of the process with customer requirements.

In summary, the SIPOC tool is a valuable asset for managers seeking to understand and analyze processes. It provides a visual representation of the process and its key components, highlighting the sequence of activities, inputs, outputs, suppliers, and customers. By leveraging SIPOC, managers can identify areas of improvement, optimize processes, and enhance customer satisfaction. It serves as a foundation for further analysis and improvement efforts, allowing managers to make data-driven decisions and drive operational excellence.

CHAPTER 3: MEASURE PHASE

OVERVIEW OF MEASURE PHASE

Alright, let's talk about the measure phase. **This is where things get real because we believe that you can't improve what you don't measure.** Makes sense, right? So, to really understand how well a process is doing, we need to gather some accurate and reliable data. This data is like the lifeline of the whole operation. It's what guides us to make informed decisions and continuously improve.

Now, the first step in the measure phase is all about planning. We have to have a solid data collection plan in place. This plan sets the stage for the whole measurement process. It tells us what kind of information we need, how to collect it, and what tools to use. Basically, it's our roadmap to success. And let me tell you, a well-executed data collection plan is gold. It ensures that we're not wasting time or resources on collecting useless data. We want the good stuff.

To make this happen, we Lean Six Sigma folks have some tricks up our sleeves. One of them is the **Process Map.** Sounds fancy, right? Well, it's actually pretty cool. This diagram gives us a clear picture view of the process and helps us figure out what data points are crucial. It's like creating a visual map of the whole process flow. This really helps us see where the key data sources are and any potential variations. We're all about connecting the dots here.

But that's not all. We've got more tools to make our lives easier. **Check sheets** come in handy when we need to collect and organize data. They keep things neat and tidy. And then there's stratified sampling. This technique lets us pick representative subsets of data, so we're not overwhelmed with information. Clever, right?

Okay, so once we have our **data collection plan** nailed down, we move on to the next step - **measurement system analysis (MSA).** This step is all about making sure the measurement system we use to collect data is top-notch. We can't have any flaws in our system, or our data will be wonky. And we definitely don't want wonky data leading us down the wrong path.

The **Gage R&R study** is our go-to tool for MSA. It's all about assessing the reliability and accuracy of our measurement system. We look at the variation caused by the person doing the measuring and the equipment used. This helps us identify any potential errors and figure out what adjustments or improvements we need to make. We're all about precision here, my friend.

Oh, and don't forget about control charts. These bad boys keep an eye on the stability and consistency of the measurement process. They make sure everything is on track. And we also have attribute agreement analysis. This helps us see if multiple appraisers agree on the measurements. We don't want any confusion, so this analysis keeps everyone on the same page.

Now, we're at the final step of the measure phase - establishing baseline performance. This is like setting a starting point, a benchmark for future improvements. It's important because we need something to compare against. It helps us see just how much we've improved. Without this baseline performance measurement, it's like flying blind.

To establish this baseline, we've got a bunch of cool tools. One of them is **statistical process control (SPC).** This baby helps us monitor and control process performance over time. It's like our watchdog, making sure everything is running smoothly. And of course, we revisit our measurement system analysis to make sure it's reliable and accurate.

Also, we can use tools such as yield, DPMO, Cp, Cpk, Pp, Ppk, Sigma level, etc. to understand and compare the baseline performance to our desired performance or industry standards. This helps us see the exact gap in performance.

So, to wrap it all up, the measure phase is a big deal in Lean Six Sigma. It's all about gathering that good data, analyzing the measurement system, and setting a baseline for future improvements. It's like taking a good hard look in the mirror and saying, "Alright, here's where we're at, and here's where we wanna be." And with this accurate and reliable data, we can take the necessary steps to improve our processes and achieve those desired outcomes.

Major Steps	• Step 4: Finalize Data Collection Plan
	• Step 5: Validate Measurement System
	• Step 6: Measure Baseline Performance
Important questions to be answered	• Have you identified the inputs (X) and the Output (Y) that needs to be measured? • Do you have an appropriate data collection plan? • Is your Measurement System Capable and adequate? • How far is your project goal from the current performance?
Main deliverables	• Baseline Performance

BASIC STATISTICS FOR SIX SIGMA

Alright, let's dive into the fascinating world of statistics. Buckle up folks, because we're about to embark on a journey that will turn numbers into stories, data into insights, and uncertainty into certainty. Ready? Let's go!

So, what the heck is statistics anyway? Well, think of it as a magical branch of mathematics that deals with the never-ending sea of data all around us. It's like having a superpower that allows us to collect, analyze, interpret, present, and organize all that mind-boggling information. And guess what? It also helps us make smart decisions. Pretty cool, right?

Now, let's uncover the secret sauce behind statistics: descriptive and inferential statistics. Descriptive statistics is like the artist that paints a vivid picture of a data set. It summarizes the information, giving us a quick snapshot of its basic characteristics. It's like looking at a beautiful landscape painting - you get a sense of what's going on, but you're not seeing the whole picture.

But wait, there's more! Inferential statistics takes us deeper into the abyss. It's like venturing into a dark cave, armed with only a tiny flashlight, searching for hidden treasures. This fancy term helps us draw conclusions about big populations based on smaller samples of data. It's all about making predictions and inferences that could change the game.

Now, let's talk about the difference between a sample and a population. Imagine you're at a party (ah, remember those?). The population is the whole party - every single person shaking their groove thing. But it's not practical to interview everyone, right? You'd scare them away! So, you just chat with a sample of people. This smaller group represents the larger population, and their thoughts and opinions are our ticket to understanding the whole shebang.

Speaking of distinguishing things, let's not confuse population characteristics with sample characteristics. Think of a population as a majestic lion, with features that define its identity. Now, the sample - it's like a tiny lion cub, all cute and cuddly. When we measure its traits, like the mean or standard deviation, we're painting a picture of that little cub, which we can, in turn, use to estimate what the big lion is like. It's like seeing the cub and imagining what the grown-up lion will look like. Roar!

Now that we've laid the groundwork, let's move on to the juicy stuff: statistical measures. These are the tools that help us analyze data and gain insights, like Sherlock Holmes solving his next case. We've got the mean, which tells us the average value of a data set. It's like finding the sweet spot in the middle of a rollercoaster ride.

Then, there's the median, the cool kid who sits right in the middle when you line up all the data. It's like spotting the Beyoncé of the group - everyone wants to be her! And let's not forget the mode, the popular kid who shows up more often than anyone else. It's like realizing that FOMO is real, and everyone's trying to do what's hot right now.

But wait, there's more! We've got the range, which tells us how far the data spreads. It's like stretching a rubber band and seeing how far it goes. And then there's the standard deviation, the rebel of the bunch. It measures how much the data points deviate from the mean. It's like trying to keep a group of rowdy kids in line!

Oh, and let's not forget about quartiles - Q1 and Q3. They're like the milestones of the data journey. Q1 is the point below which 25% of the data falls, and Q3 is the point below which 75% is hiding. These two buddies help us calculate the inter-quartile range, which gives us the scoop on the middle 50% of the data. It's like finding the juicy meat of a sandwich between two fluffy buns.

Alright, now that we're done with this statistical feast, let's move on to the fancy stuff. Picture this: normal distribution, a beautiful bell-shaped curve that's all about balance and harmony. It pops up everywhere in statistics, like encountering a unicorn on your morning walk. It's defined by its mean and standard deviation, magical numbers that breathe life into the curve.

And get this - the standard normal distribution is like the queen of all distributions. It's a special case where the mean is 0 and the standard deviation is 1. It's like entering a secret garden where everything is perfectly in place. We use this queen to help us make powerful calculations and test some mind-boggling hypotheses. She's a real game-changer.

But wait, what about control limits? Imagine a superhero with an invisible force field. Well, control limits are just that. They're like boundaries that determine whether a process is behaving or going off the rails. They define the expected range of behavior, so if any data points step outside, we know something fishy is going on. It's like having a radar that alerts us to trouble. Batman would be proud.

And speaking of rules, let me introduce you to the 68.27 - 95.45 - 99.73 rule of probability - or the empirical rule, as I like to call it. It's like having a secret formula that tells us how much of the data falls within certain ranges. Nearly 70% is within one standard deviation, around 95% within two, and an astonishing 99.73% within three. It's like cracking the code to a hidden treasure chest.

Last but not least, let's not forget our old friend probability. It's like a weather forecast that tells us the chances of rain. Probability helps us measure the likelihood of an event happening. It's what keeps us sane when making big decisions. After all, we all need a little certainty in our lives, don't we?

So now you know, my friends. Statistics is like a thrilling rollercoaster ride that takes us from basic concepts to complex analysis. It opens up a world of possibilities, where numbers become stories and data becomes our guide. It's the backbone of Lean Six Sigma, guiding us towards operational excellence and helping us make the best damn decisions out there.

So, let's embrace the power of statistics and embark on this adventure together. It's time to unleash our inner Sherlock Holmes, our secret unicorn, and our superhero self. Let's paint our canvas with numbers, unlock the secrets of data, and ride the waves of uncertainty. We've got this!

Statistical Terms	Explanation	Numerical Summary	Graphical Summary / Remarks
Descriptive Statistics	Provides a clear and concise summary of data collected over a period of time.	Mean: 10 min. Standard deviation: 1.25 min. Range: 6 to 13 min. N: 50	Histogram of wait times
Inferential statistics	Predicting the population characteristics using the sample characteristics	-	-
Mean	A single value representing the center of the data. Otherwise mean is the sum of all	The waiting time of five customer in a store are: 4, 3, 5, 2, and 3 minutes. The	On an average, a customer waits 3.4 minutes for service at the store

	observations divided by the number of observations	mean waiting time is: $4 + 3 + 5 + 2 + 3 =$ 17/5 = 3.4 min	
Median	The middle of the range of data: half the observations are less than or equal to it and half the observations are greater than or equal to it. If the data set contains an odd number of values, then, median = value of middle term value. If the data set contains an even number of values, median = average of middle two terms	For example, the median of data set 22,29,33,34,36 is 33 For example, the median of data set 22,29,33,34,36,43 is average of 33 and 34, which is 33.5	Whenever a data set contains outlier or skewed data, Median is the best measure of central tendency. It is not sensitive to extreme data values.
Mode	The value that occurs most frequently in a set of observations is called Mode	In the data set 3,5,6,6,6,6,7,7,7,7,8, 8,8,8,8,8,8,8,9,9,9, 9,9,9,10,10. The mode is 8	
Variance	A measure of dispersion, which is the extent to which a data set or distribution is scattered around its mean.	$$s^2 = \frac{\sum(x - \bar{x})^2}{n - 1}$$	Variance (s^2) is a squared quantity. For example, a sample of waiting times in a bank have a mean of 15 minutes and a variance of 9 minutes^2. Variance is often converted to standard deviation (s). A variance of 9 minutes^2 is equivalent to a standard deviation of 3 minutes.
Standard deviation	Standard deviation estimates the "average" distance of the individual observations from the mean.	$$s = \sqrt{\frac{\sum(x - \bar{x})^2}{n - 1}}$$	The greater the standard deviation, the greater the spread in the data.
Range	The difference between the largest and smallest data values.	The waiting time of five customers in a bank are: 4,3,5,2 & 3. R = 5-2 = 3 min	Waiting time ranges from 2 to 5 minutes
Quartiles	Quartiles are values that divide a sample of data into four equal parts. **First quartile (Q1):** 25% of the data are less than or equal to	For a dataset of 6,8,15,35,38,44,44,4 5,47,50 Q1 = 13.25;	

	this value. **Second quartile (Q2):** The median. 50% of the data are less than or equal to this value. **Third quartile (Q3):** 75% of the data are less than or equal to this value. **Interquartile range:** The distance between the first and third quartiles (Q3-Q1); thus, it spans the middle 50% of the data.	Q2 = Median = 41 Q3 = 45.5; IQR = 32.25	
Normal distribution	A bell-shaped curve that is symmetric about its mean. The normal distribution is the most common statistical distribution because approximate normality arises naturally in many situations. The normal distribution is also known as the Gaussian distribution. The mean (μ) and the standard deviation (σ) are the two parameters that define the normal distribution.	Approximately, 68% of observations are within +/- 1 standard deviation of the mean; 95% are within +/- 2 standards deviations of the mean; and 99% are within +/- 3 standard deviations of the mean.	
Probability Distribution Plot	Probability Distribution Plots can help you: Clearly visualize distribution shapes. See how changing a parameter value affects the curve Compare two different distributions to see how well one approximates another. View the probabilities associated with specific areas under the curve.	This graph actually plots probability density functions (PDF) which describes the likelihood of each data value. Typically, you specify the distribution, parameter values, and, optionally, a region of interest to shade under the curve.	

ACTIVITY - 5: VARIANCE (S^2) AND STD. DEVIATION (S)

Runs scored by Mohit Sharma in 10 consecutive innings in a recent T20 series was recorded. Compute the variance and standard deviation of his batting performance and write your inference.

Innings	1	2	3	4	5	6	7	8	9	10
Runs	38	48	42	51	69	58	22	8	59	44

Data (X_i)	Difference between X_i and mean ($X_i - X$ bar)	Squared difference ($X_i - X$ bar)^2
Mean =	**Sum of deviations from the mean =**	**Sum of squared deviations =**

Variance (S^2) = Sum of squared deviations / (n-1) =

Sample standard deviation (S) = Square root of Variance =

INFERENCE:

Mohit Sharma's expected score in the next batch:

Mohit Sharma's expected batting average in the next series:

DATA COLLECTION PLAN

To begin with, it is important to understand the different types of data that we may encounter in our projects. Two main categories of data exist: continuous and discrete. Continuous data refers to measurements that can take on any value within a range, such as time, temperature, or length. On the other hand, discrete data consists of finite values and is often represented in countable units, such as the number of defects, customer complaints, or errors.

Before diving into data collection, it is essential to establish an **operational definition** for the metric you are evaluating. Operational definitions clarify what exactly is being measured, ensuring consistency and accuracy throughout the process. By clearly defining the criteria, you eliminate the possibility of misinterpretation or subjectivity, enabling smooth data collection and analysis.

Once the operational definition is in place, it is time to determine the appropriate sample size. Sample size selection is crucial as it affects the reliability and validity of your conclusions. If the sample size is too small, the data may not accurately represent the true state of the process, leading to incorrect decisions. Conversely, an unnecessarily large sample can be time-consuming and resource-intensive. To determine the ideal sample size, you need to consider factors such as the desired level of precision, confidence level, and variability of the data. Various statistical formulas and sample size calculators are available to assist you in this process.

Next, you must decide on the **sampling technique** that aligns with your specific needs. Two commonly used techniques are probability sampling and non-probability sampling. Probability sampling ensures that each item in the population has an equal chance of being selected, guaranteeing a representative sample. Examples of probability sampling methods include simple random sampling, stratified sampling, and cluster sampling. On the other hand, non-probability sampling does not involve random selection and may introduce sampling bias; however, it can be more convenient and cost-effective in certain situations. Common non-probability sampling techniques include convenience sampling, judgment sampling, and quota sampling.

The choice of the most appropriate data collection method depends on several factors, including the goal of the project, the characteristics of the process, and the resources available. Some commonly used data collection methods include surveys, interviews, direct observation, and existing data analysis. Surveys are a popular method for collecting large amounts of data quickly and efficiently and can be administered through various channels, such as online questionnaires or paper surveys. Interviews, on the other hand, provide an opportunity for in-depth exploration and clarification of responses. They are particularly useful when seeking detailed insights from stakeholders or subject matter experts.

Direct observation involves physically witnessing the process or activity being studied. This method is valuable when relying on objective data and minimizes the chances of biased responses or misinterpretations. Existing data analysis entails leveraging data that has already been collected for other purposes but can provide relevant insights for the current project. Examples of existing data sources include customer complaints, customer feedback, or financial records.

While collecting data, it is crucial to focus on accuracy, reliability, and confidentiality. Accuracy ensures that the data represents the true state of the process without errors or biases. Reliability refers to the consistency of the measurements, necessitating appropriate training and standardization procedures among data collectors. Additionally, confidentiality is of utmost importance to protect sensitive information and ensure the ethical handling of data. Instituting measures to guarantee data privacy provides contributors with a sense of security and promotes transparency in the data collection process.

In conclusion, a well-designed data collection plan forms the foundation for meaningful insights and effective decision-making in a Lean Six Sigma project. This subchapter has provided an overview of various considerations when creating a data collection plan, including data types, operational definitions, sample size determination, sampling techniques, and data collection methods. It is crucial to approach data collection with a systematic and well-thought-out plan to ensure accurate, reliable, and confidential data. By doing so, you will be equipped with the key information needed to drive process improvement, achieve operational excellence, and ultimately deliver enhanced value to both your organization and its stakeholders.

MEASUREMENT SYSTEM ANALYSIS

As we delve further into the world of Lean Six Sigma, it becomes crucial to ensure the accuracy and reliability of our measurement systems. After all, the quality of our data and analysis depends on the quality of our measurements. In this chapter, we will discuss the methods used to assess the capability of a measurement system by estimating the measurement error. Two commonly used techniques for this purpose are Gage R&R study and Attribute Agreement Analysis.

Gage R&R Study for Continuous Data:

When dealing with continuous data, such as measurements on a scale, it is important to evaluate the variation introduced by the measurement system itself. This is where the Gage R&R study comes into play. This study involves the participation of multiple operators who measure the same part multiple times using the same measurement system. The results are then analyzed to estimate the various sources of variation and assess the capability of the measurement system.

To conduct a Gage R&R study, a sample of 10 parts is selected that represents the range of variation expected in the process. Each operator measures each part multiple times, typically at least three replications. The measurements are recorded in a data sheet for further analysis.

The analysis of the Gage R&R study involves estimating three key components of variation: the Total Variation (TV), the Equipment Variation (EV), and the Operator Variation (OV). The Total Variation represents the total variation in the measurements, which is the sum of the Equipment and Operator Variations. The Equipment Variation, also known as repeatability error reflects the measurement error introduced by the same measurement system, while the Operator Variation, also known as reproducibility error captures the measurement error due to differences among measurement systems.

The Gage R&R value is calculated as the ratio of the combined variation due to Equipment and Operator to the Total Variation. A Gage R&R value of less than 10% is generally considered acceptable, indicating a reliable and capable measurement system. Values higher than 10% indicate that a significant portion of the total variation is due to the measurement system itself, which can lead to erroneous conclusions and decisions.

Attribute Agreement Analysis for Attribute Data:

When dealing with attribute data, which consists of qualitative or categorical values, we use Attribute Agreement Analysis. Attribute data often involves subjective judgments or evaluations, such as pass/fail or good/bad ratings. Attribute Agreement Analysis is used to assess the consistency and agreement among different evaluators or observers for a given attribute.

In an Attribute Agreement Analysis, a sample of items is selected, and each item is evaluated by multiple evaluators independently. The evaluations are recorded, and the data is tabulated to assess the level of agreement among the evaluators.

The most commonly used measure of agreement in Attribute Agreement Analysis is the percent agreement or accuracy. This represents the proportion of evaluations that are in agreement among the evaluators. A team accuracy of 90% is typically preferred, indicating a high level of consistency and agreement among the evaluators. Values lower than 90% suggest a lack of agreement and inconsistency among evaluators, which can lead to unreliable and biased results.

Conclusion:

In conclusion, the accuracy and reliability of our measurement systems are crucial for successful Lean Six Sigma initiatives. Measurement System Analysis allows us to assess the capability of our measurement systems and estimate the measurement error. Gage R&R study is used for continuous data, while Attribute Agreement Analysis is used for attribute data. A Gage R&R value of less than 10% is preferred, indicating a reliable measurement system, while a team accuracy of 90% is preferred for Attribute Agreement Analysis. By diligently evaluating and improving our measurement systems, we can ensure the quality and integrity of our data, leading to more effective problem-solving and process improvement.

BASELINE PERFORMANCE

Calculating baseline performance requires the use of various tools and metrics, such as **Yield, Defects Per Million Opportunities (DPMO), Cp, Cpk, Pp, Ppk, and Sigma level.** Each of these metrics provides valuable insights into the organization's performance and process capability.

To begin, let's explore the calculation of **Yield.** Yield is a measure of the percentage of defect-free products or services produced by a process. It quantifies how effectively a process meets customer requirements. To calculate Yield, we simply divide the number of defect-free outputs by the total number of outputs. For example, if a process produces 800 defect-free units out of 1000, the Yield would be 80% (800/1000).

Next, we move on to **Defects Per Million Opportunities (DPMO).** DPMO provides a standardized measure of process defects. It is calculated by multiplying the total number of defects by one million and dividing it by the total number of opportunities for defects. For instance, if a process results in 50 defects and has a total of 10,000 opportunities for defects, the DPMO would be 5,000 (50 * 1,000,000/10,000).

Cp (Potential Process Capability Ratio) and **Cpk (Process Capability Index)** are metrics used to assess whether a process is capable of meeting customer requirements. Cp measures the potential capability of a process, while Cpk takes into account any deviation from the customer's specification limits. These metrics provide an indication of process performance.

To calculate Cp, we divide the difference between the upper and lower specification limits by six times the process standard deviation. The formula would be (USL - LSL) / (6 * σ). If a process has an upper specification limit (USL) of 40 and a lower specification limit (LSL) of 20, with a process standard deviation (σ) of 5, we can calculate Cp as (40 - 20) / (6 * 5), which equals 0.67.

Moving on to Cpk, we consider the capability index with respect to the mean. Cpk takes into account both the process capability and any deviation from the target value or mean. To calculate Cpk, we use the formula min [Cpu, Cpl], where Cpu is equal to (USL - mean) / (3 * σ) and Cpl is equal to (mean - LSL) / (3 * σ). The result reflects the capability of the process in relation to the specification limits. It is to be noted that, the 'σ' used for calculation of Cp and Cpk is the standard deviation within subgroups.

Another important metric is **Pp (Potential Process Performance)**, which is similar to Cp and assesses process capability. However, Pp does not take into account any deviation from the target value. To calculate Pp, we use the formula (USL - LSL) / (6 * σ). For example, if a process has an upper specification limit (USL) of 40, a lower specification limit (LSL) of 20, and an overall standard deviation (σ) of 5, Pp would be (40 - 20) / (6 * 5), resulting in a value of 0.67.

Lastly, we come to **Ppk (Process Performance Index)**, which combines process performance with any deviation from the target value. Ppk considers both the process capability and the deviation from the mean. Ppk is calculated using the formula Min [Ppu, Ppl], where Ppu is equal to (USL - mean) / (3 * σ) and Ppl is equal to (mean - LSL) / (3 * σ). The result provides an assessment of process performance against the specification limits. It is to be noted that, the 'σ' used for calculation of Pp and Ppk is the overall standard deviation of the data collected.

Sigma level (Z) is a metric that quantifies process performance in terms of the standard deviation. It is a measure of process capability and variation. Higher sigma levels indicate better process performance. Sigma level can be calculated using the formula (USL - mean) / σ, where USL is the upper specification limit.

In conclusion, baseline performance is crucial for organizations looking to implement Lean Six Sigma methodologies. Calculating baseline performance provides a solid foundation for identifying opportunities for improvement and measuring progress. By utilizing tools such as Yield, DPMO, Cp, Cpk, Pp, Ppk, and Sigma level, organizations can gain valuable insights into process capability and performance. These metrics allow managers and leaders to make data-driven decisions and drive operational excellence across various domains. Through continuous improvement efforts guided by these metrics, organizations can enhance their overall efficiency, quality, and customer satisfaction.

ACTIVITY – 6: BASELINE PERFORMANCE FOR CONTINUOUS DATA

1. We have specified that the temperature in the training room should be 21 ± 3 degrees. The average room temperature is 22 and standard deviation is 2. What is the sigma level?

Mean: 22;   Standard Dev: 2;   LSL: 18;   USL: 24

DPMO:181405.4;   Sigma Level (LT) 0.91   Sigma Level (ST)   2.41

2. A manufacturer wants to assess the performance of a shear cutting machine. They have audited 100 16" length rods. The acceptable specification is 16 ± 0.5. Process mean = 15.992; Process standard deviation = 0.246. Compute the Zst value.

Input specification limits (LSL=15.5; USL=16.5), mean and standard deviation values in the sigma level calculator. Sigma Level (LT) = 1.73   Sigma Level (ST) = 3.23

3. An insurance company processes refund receipts for their customers. The time to process should be less than 30 minutes and the customer expects that the invoices should be processed within 30 minutes. What is the probability of processing the refund of bills within 30 minutes? Compute the Zst. (Refer data: Refund.mtw)

4. In a diagnostics lab, the maximum time allowed to complete a Diabetic test is 90 minutes. The lab analyst randomly selected a sample and recorded the time taken to carry out each test. Please compute the current sigma level (Zst). (Refer data: Diabetic Test.mtw)

5. The diameter of the tennis ball should be between 224mm and 229mm. An operator collected a sample of 100 tennis balls and recorded the diameter. Compute Zst. (Refer data: Tennis Balls.mtw)

ACTIVITY – 7: BASELINE PERFORMANCE FOR DISCRETE DATA

1. 500 health reports from a diagnostic laboratory were inspected for 5 different characteristics before dispatch. We observed 224 defects. What is the sigma level?

Defects = 224; Sample = 500;

OFE = 5; TOFE = 2500; DPO = 0.09; DPMO = 89600;

Z_{lt} = 1.34; Z_{st} = 2.84

2. 1000 televisions were inspected. We observed 116 defects. What is the sigma level?

Defects = 116; Sample = 1000

OFE = Unknown; DPU = 0.116; DPMO = 109525

Z_{lt} = 1.23; Z_{st} = 2.73

3. 1000 garments were inspected. 31 were defective. What is the sigma level?

Defectives = 31; Sample = 1000

Yield = 96.90%; DPMO = 31000

Z_{lt} = 1.87; Z_{st} = 3.37

4. Laptops are being inspected to check whether the following components are functional. RAM, Motherboard, Screen, Hard disk, Bluetooth, DVD-Drive and Memory Slot. 500 laptops are inspected and 119 defects are observed. What is Zst?

5. The circuit board of projector is inspected. The OFE is unknown. 1000 projectors are inspected and 43 defects are obtained. What is Zst?

6. Phone calls are recorded at a call centre and later evaluated. A sample of 200 calls are heard by the quality representatives and evaluated based on a Call Quality checklist. There are 14 opportunities for error in each call. 284 defects were observed in the sample of 200 calls. What is Zst?

7. 2000 dishes are inspected. 42 are defectives. What is Zst?

ACTIVITY – 8: TRADITIONAL YIELD, FPY, RTY

1. In a process of inflating tires on scooters in an assembly, a study revealed that of 360 tires that went through the tire inflation process during a day's production, 354 were later found to have the pressure within the required specification limits. Tire after inflation is immediately inspected to ensure that it meets the required pressure specification limits. Inspection detected 94 tires that do not comply with pressure specification. The operators corrected 88 tires, leaving 6 that could not be brought back to specification and therefore scrapped.

Metric	Formula	Result	Comments
Traditional Yield	Y = Output / Input		
First Pass Yield (FPY)	Y = (Output – Rework) / Input		

2. In a process there are 4 steps namely A, B, C and D. Calculate the first Pass Yield, Stepwise. Also find out the rolled throughput yield.

STEP	INPUT	OUTPUT	REWORKED	SCRAPPED	FPY
A	734	698	16	36	
B	698	655	7	43	
C	655	649	3	6	
D	649	645	10	4	

ROLED THROUGHPUT YIELD (RTY)

RTY = (Final Output – Total reworked units) / Initial Input = 82.97

Yield Type	STEP-A	STEP-B	STEP-3	STEP-4	RTY
FPY	**92.91**	**92.83**	**98.62**	**97.84**	**83.22**

Alternate Formula: RTY = $FPY_A * FPY_B * FPY_C * FPY_D$

3. In a process there are 4 steps namely A, B, C and D. Calculate the Rolled Throughput Yield

STEP	INPUT	OUTPUT	FPY	RTY
A	734	698	95.09	
B	698	655	93.83	
C	655	649	99.08	
D	649	645	99.38	

ACTIVITY – 9: BASELINE PERFORMANCE (CAPABILITY INDICES)

<table>
<tr><td>

1. **For an electronic manufacturing process, the specification for current flow is 100 ± 10 milliamperes. The process average and standard deviation are 107.0 and 1.5 respectively. Compute C_p, C_{pk}**

</td></tr>
<tr><td>

CUSTOMER TOLERANCE = USL – LSL; PROCESS TOLERANCE = 6σ

</td></tr>
<tr><td>

C_p = Customer Tolerance / Process Tolerance = (USL – LSL) / 6σ

</td></tr>
<tr><td>

Cp = (110-90)/6*1.5 = 20/9 = 2.22

</td></tr>
<tr><td colspan="2">

C_{pk} = Min (C_{pu}, C_{pl}); = Min {(USL – Mean) / (3σ), (Mean - LSL) / (3σ)}

</td></tr>
<tr><td>

C_{pu} = (110 – 107) / (3*1.5) = 0.66

</td><td>

C_{pl} = (107 - 90) / (3*1.5) = 3.77

</td></tr>
<tr><td>

C_{pk} = Min (C_{pu}, C_{pl}) = 0.66

</td></tr>
<tr><td>

INFERENCE:

</td></tr>
</table>

<table>
<tr><td>

2. **An extrusion die is used to produce aluminium rods. The diameter of the rods is a critical quality characteristic. Specifications on the rods are 0.5035 ± 0.0010 inch. The process average is 0.5031 and standard deviation is 0.0003. Compute Cp, Cpk**

</td></tr>
<tr><td>

CUSTOMER TOLERANCE = USL – LSL; PROCESS TOLERANCE = 6σ

</td></tr>
<tr><td>

Cp = Customer Tolerance / Process Tolerance = (USL – LSL) / 6σ

</td></tr>
<tr><td>

Cp = (0.0020)/6*0.0003 = 1.11

</td></tr>
<tr><td colspan="2">

Cpk = Min (Cpu, Cpl); = Min {(USL – Mean) / (3σ), (Mean - LSL) / (3σ)}

</td></tr>
<tr><td>

Cpu = (0.5045 – 0.5031) / (3*0.0003) = 1.55

</td><td>

Cpl = (0.5031 – 0.5025) / (3*0.0003) = 0.66

</td></tr>
<tr><td>

Cpk = Mln (Cpu, Cpl) = 0.66

</td></tr>
<tr><td>

INFERENCE:

</td></tr>
</table>

Fill up the following table and draw inference about Process Capability

Case	USL	LSL	Target	Process Mean	Est. Std. Deviation	Specification Width	Process Width	C_p	C_{pu}	C_{pl}	C_{pk}
1	24	18	21	23	0.5						
2	24	18	21	22	0.5						
3	24	18	21	21	0.5						
4	24	18	21	20	0.5						
5	24	18	21	19	0.5						

Write your inference in the below table

Case	C_p	C_{pk}	Process Stable?	Process Capable?	Action Needed
1	2	0.66			
2	2	1.33			
3	2	2			
4	2	1.33			
5	2	0.66			

CHAPTER 4: ANALYZE PHASE

OVERVIEW OF ANALYZE PHASE

The first step in the Analyze phase is to identify the possible factors that could be contributing to the problem. This involves conducting a detailed analysis of the process and gathering relevant data to understand its current state. As a Master Black Belt Certified Six Sigma practitioner, I have utilized various tools and techniques such as 5S deployment, Kaizen, Statistical Process Control, Measurement System Analysis, and Process Capability to accurately identify these factors.

Identifying the potentially critical factors is the next step in the Analyze phase. Once we have identified the possible factors, we need to validate their significance in relation to the problem at hand. This involves conducting further data analysis and statistical tests to determine the degree of influence each factor has on the process output. Through my years of experience, I have gained a deep understanding of hypothesis testing, regression analysis, and design of experiments, which enables me to accurately identify the critical factors and their impact on the process.

Validating the root causes is another crucial step in the Analyze phase. It involves further investigation and confirmation of the factors identified earlier. This can be done through additional data collection, observation, and consultation with subject matter experts. It is essential to gather accurate and reliable data to ensure that the root causes are correctly identified and understood. As a seasoned consultant, I have honed my skills in customer need analysis, quality function deployment, and other research methods to validate these root causes effectively.

One of the primary goals of the Analyze phase is to verify the sufficiency of the root causes. This step ensures that the identified root causes are indeed the major contributors to the problem and that addressing them will lead to significant improvements in the process. To verify the sufficiency, we must thoroughly examine the relationship between the root causes and the process output. This may involve conducting additional experiments or simulations to measure the percentage contribution of each root cause. By quantifying the impact of each factor, we gain a better understanding of which areas require the most attention and resources.

The steps in the Analyze phase are vital in providing the solution generation team with accurate and reliable information. This information serves as the foundation for developing effective solutions to the identified problem. Armed with a clear understanding of the root causes and their relationship with the process output, the team can confidently move forward in generating solutions that address the underlying issues.

By gathering accurate data and assessing the reliability of our measurement system, we ensure that the information we base our decisions on is valid and trustworthy. This instills confidence in the team and stakeholders, as the solutions developed will be backed by solid evidence and analysis. The Analyze phase is not merely about identifying problems; it is about understanding them at a deep level and developing solutions that have a lasting impact on the organization.

In conclusion, the Analyze phase is a critical component of the DMAIC methodology. It provides us with the necessary tools and techniques to identify and validate the root causes of problems in our processes. By following the three important steps of identifying possible factors, identifying potentially critical factors and validating them, and verifying the sufficiency of root causes, we gather accurate data and ensure the solution generation team has the correct information. With this information, we can move forward confidently to develop effective solutions that address the underlying issues.

Major Steps	• Step 7: Identify Possible and Potential X Factors
	• Step 8: Validate Critical Factors
	• Step 9: Verify Sufficiency of Critical Factors
Important questions to be answered	• Have you identified the sources of waste, risk and variation? • Have you identified the critical X factors that affect project Y (CTQ)? • Have you statistically validated the root causes of the problem? • Have the validated X factors been sufficient to realize the targeted improvement in Y?
Main deliverables	• Validated Root Causes

LIST POSSIBLE CAUSE FACTORS

To list all possible cause factors, we can employ various tools and techniques such as Brainstorming, Why-Why Analysis, and Cause and Effect diagram. These tools enable the team to systematically explore and consider multiple perspectives to ensure a comprehensive identification of potential causes. Let's discuss each of these tools and their application in detail.

Brainstorming is a powerful technique for generating a large number of ideas or potential causes in a short amount of time. As a Master Black Belt Certified Six Sigma practitioner, I have extensively utilized brainstorming sessions to facilitate discussions with cross-functional teams to identify all possible X factors. In these sessions, team members are encouraged to freely express their thoughts and ideas without any judgment or criticism, fostering a supportive and creative environment. I believe in the power of collective intelligence and have witnessed firsthand how brainstorming can uncover unique insights and perspectives that might have otherwise been overlooked.

Another effective tool for exploring potential causes is the **Why-Why Analysis.** This technique, rooted in the principle of asking successive why questions, allows us to dig deeper into the underlying causes of a problem. By repeatedly asking 'why' for each identified factor, we can trace back the root causes and uncover the true sources of the performance gap. I find the Why-Why Analysis particularly helpful in challenging assumptions and exploring different angles to gain a holistic understanding of the problem at hand.

The third tool, the **Cause-and-Effect diagram** (also known as the Ishikawa or Fishbone diagram), provides a structured approach for organizing and categorizing potential cause factors. This diagram allows us to visually represent the cause-and-effect relationships in a hierarchical manner, making it easier to analyze the contributing factors. The main categories commonly used in a Cause-and-Effect diagram include People, Process, Materials, Machines, Measurement, and Environment. By systematically brainstorming within each category, we can uncover a comprehensive list of potential causes.

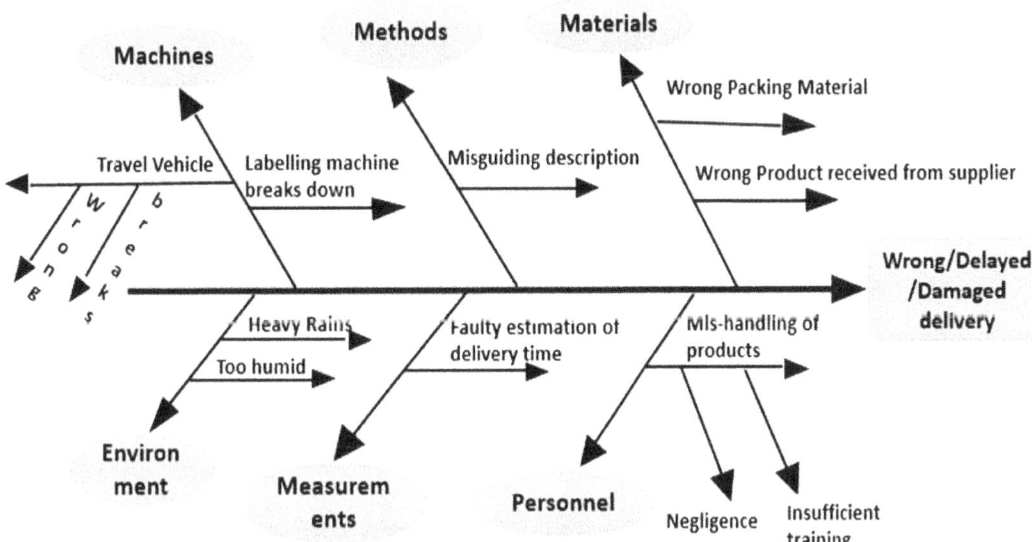

When applying these tools, it is essential to involve a diverse group of stakeholders who possess expertise and insights from different areas. By leveraging the collective expertise and knowledge of the team, we can ensure thorough coverage of all possible cause factors.

Now, let me take you through a step-by-step guide on how to effectively use these tools to list all possible X factors for the identified performance gap:

1. Gather the right team: Assemble a cross-functional team that includes individuals from various departments or areas related to the process under investigation. This diversity will enhance the team's ability to identify a broad range of potential causes.

2. Define the problem statement: Clearly articulate the performance gap or problem that needs to be addressed. This will ensure that all team members have a clear understanding of the scope and context of the project.

3. Brainstorming session: Conduct a brainstorming session where team members generate ideas and potential causes without any judgment or criticism. Encourage everyone to freely contribute their thoughts, promoting a culture of open communication and collaboration.

4. Capture the ideas: As the team generates ideas, record them in a visible and easily accessible format. This could be a whiteboard, a flipchart, or a digital platform, depending on the preferences and resources available.

5. Analyze and categorize: Once the brainstorming session is complete, review the list of potential causes and categorize them based on the different dimensions of the Cause-and-Effect diagram (People, Process, Materials, Machines, Measurement, and Environment). This categorization will help organize the causes and facilitate a more structured analysis.

6. Apply the Why-Why Analysis: For each potential cause identified, apply the Why-Why Analysis technique. Continuously ask 'why' for each cause until the team reaches the root cause(s). This iterative process will unveil hidden factors that may not be immediately apparent.

7. Prioritize potential causes: Assess the potential causes based on their impact and likelihood. This prioritization will help determine which causes require further investigation and analysis in the subsequent phases of the Lean Six Sigma project.

By following this step-by-step guide, we can ensure a thorough exploration and identification of all possible cause factors. Remember, the objective in the Measure phase is to establish a strong foundation for subsequent analysis and improvement. By utilizing tools such as Brainstorming, Why-Why Analysis, and the Cause-and-Effect diagram, we can maximize the team's collective intelligence and systematically list all the X factors contributing to the observed performance gap.

In conclusion, identifying all possible cause factors for the gap in performance requires a structured approach and the application of various tools and techniques. By employing Brainstorming, Why-Why Analysis, and the Cause-and-Effect diagram, we can ensure a comprehensive exploration of potential causes, enabling the team to address the root causes effectively. So, let us leverage these tools to dive deep into the analysis phase and unravel the underlying factors to bridge the performance gap.

IMPACT CONTROL MATRIX

To provide some context, a Lean Six Sigma project involves identifying and addressing the root causes of a problem or inefficiency within an organization. These root causes are the factors that, when controlled or improved, can have a significant impact on the overall performance and success of the process. However, not all causes are equally important. Some causes have a greater impact on the desired outcomes, while others may have a negligible or even negative effect.

The Impact Control matrix allows managers to visually rank and prioritize the causes based on their significance. It consists of four quadrants, each representing a different level of impact and control. By placing causes within these quadrants, managers can identify the factors that require immediate attention, as well as those that can be addressed at a later stage or even disregarded entirely.

High Control Low Impact	High Control High Impact
Low Control Low Impact	Low Control High Impact

To effectively utilize the Impact Control matrix, there are three key steps that managers need to follow:

Step 1: Identifying the Potential Causes

The first step is to identify all the potential causes that could be contributing to the problem at hand. This involves conducting a thorough analysis, gathering data, and brainstorming with the project team. It is important to have a comprehensive list of causes to ensure that all possible factors are considered. This step also helps in avoiding any oversight or bias towards certain causes.

Step 2: Evaluating the Impact of Causes

Once the potential causes have been identified, the next step is to assess their impact on the desired outcomes. This requires collecting and analyzing data to determine the extent to which each cause influences the performance of the process. The impact can be measured in terms of cost, time, quality, customer satisfaction, or any other relevant metric. By quantifying the impact, managers can objectively compare and prioritize causes.

Step 3: Assessing the Controllability of Causes

After evaluating the impact, the next step is to assess the controllability of each cause. Controllability refers to the degree to which the cause can be controlled or influenced by the organization. Some causes may be beyond the organization's control, such as external factors or market conditions. Others may be within the organization's influence, such as process parameters or employee behavior. By assessing the controllability, managers can determine the level of effort and resources required to address each cause.

Once the impact and controllability of causes have been assessed, managers can plot them on the Impact Control matrix. The matrix consists of four quadrants: Vital Few, Promising Few, Useful Many, and Trivial Many. Let's explore each quadrant in detail:

1. Vital Few:

The Vital Few quadrant represents the causes that have a high impact on the desired outcomes and are within the organization's control. These causes are the most critical and require immediate attention. They have the potential to significantly improve the performance of the process if addressed effectively. Managers should allocate resources and prioritize improvement efforts towards these causes to ensure maximum impact on the desired outcomes.

2. Promising Few:

The Promising Few quadrant includes causes that have a high impact on the desired outcomes but are beyond the organization's control. These causes may be influenced by external factors or stakeholders outside the organization's scope. While the organization may not have direct control over these causes, it can still work towards mitigating their impact. Collaboration with external stakeholders, strategic partnerships, or lobbying for policy changes are some ways to address these causes indirectly.

3. Useful Many:

The Useful Many quadrant consists of causes that have a low impact on the desired outcomes but are within the organization's control. These causes may not significantly affect the overall performance of the process, but addressing them can still lead to incremental improvements. Managers should allocate resources and prioritize improvement efforts towards these causes but place less emphasis compared to the Vital Few quadrant.

4. Trivial Many:

The Trivial Many quadrant represents causes that have a low impact on the desired outcomes and are beyond the organization's control. These causes can be considered insignificant and do not warrant immediate attention or resources. Managers should minimize or disregard efforts towards addressing these causes as they do not contribute significantly to the overall success of the process.

By categorizing and prioritizing causes using the Impact Control matrix, managers can effectively deploy their resources and efforts towards the most critical factors. This helps in streamlining the improvement process, ensuring that the organization focuses on the causes that will have the most significant impact.

Furthermore, the Impact Control matrix also facilitates communication and alignment among the project team and stakeholders. It provides a clear visual representation of the causes, allowing all involved parties to understand and agree on the priorities. This alignment is crucial for ensuring a coordinated effort towards achieving the desired outcomes.

In conclusion, the Impact Control matrix is a valuable tool in Lean Six Sigma that helps managers separate vital cause factors from trivial ones. By following a step-by-step process of identifying potential causes, evaluating their impact, and assessing their controllability, managers can effectively categorize and prioritize the causes using the matrix. This ensures that the organization focuses its resources and efforts on the factors that will have the greatest impact on the desired outcomes. By leveraging the Impact Control matrix, managers can improve the efficiency and effectiveness of their improvement projects, leading to enhanced performance and success.

HYPOTHESIS TESTING FOR ROOT CAUSE VALIDATION

In the world of Lean Six Sigma, data is the lifeblood that informs decision-making and drives process improvement. However, simply collecting data is not enough. We must also validate our assumptions and ensure that the data we have collected supports our conclusions. This is where hypothesis testing comes into play.

Hypothesis testing is a statistical technique that allows us to make inferences about a population based on a sample. It allows us to test whether a particular assumption or claim about the population is supported by the data we have collected. By doing so, we can make more confident and data-driven decisions.

There are two types of hypotheses in hypothesis testing: **null hypotheses (H0) and alternative hypotheses (Ha).** The null hypothesis represents the status quo or the assumption that there is no significant difference or relationship between variables. The alternative hypothesis, on the other hand, suggests that there is indeed a significant difference or relationship.

To test these hypotheses, we follow a step-by-step procedure. First, we state our null and alternative hypotheses based on the question we are trying to answer. We then collect a sample from the population and calculate a test statistic, which is a numerical summary of the sample data. The test statistic is used to determine the likelihood of observing the sample data if the null hypothesis is true.

Next, we determine the **significance level,** also known as alpha (α), which represents the probability of rejecting the null hypothesis when it is actually true. Commonly used significance levels are 0.05 and 0.01, but they can vary depending on the situation and the level of risk we are willing to accept.

The next step is to compare the test statistic to the critical values associated with the chosen significance level. These critical values are obtained from statistical tables or calculated using statistical software. If the test statistic falls within the acceptance region, we fail to reject the null hypothesis. However, if it falls within the rejection region, we reject the null hypothesis in favor of the alternative hypothesis.

It is important to note that rejecting the null hypothesis does not prove the alternative hypothesis to be true. It simply suggests that the data we have collected provides evidence against the null hypothesis. Further analysis and experimentation may be needed to establish the validity of the alternative hypothesis.

There are several statistical tests commonly used in hypothesis testing, depending on the nature of the data and the question we are trying to answer. Some of these tests include the t-test, chi-square test, ANOVA, and regression analysis. Each test has its own assumptions and requirements, which must be met for the results to be valid.

One key consideration in hypothesis testing is the sample size. **A larger sample size increases the power of the test and makes it more likely to detect a true difference or relationship.** Therefore, it is important to determine an appropriate sample size before conducting the test. This can be done using power calculations or by consulting existing literature or expert knowledge.

Another important concept in hypothesis testing is **statistical significance.** Statistical significance refers to the likelihood of obtaining the observed results by chance alone, assuming that the null hypothesis is true. A result is considered statistically significant if the **p-value**, which represents the probability of obtaining the observed results or more extreme, is less than the chosen significance level.

However, statistical significance should not be confused with practical significance. While a result may be statistically significant, it may not have a meaningful impact on the process or the business. It is important to consider both statistical and practical significance when interpreting the results of a hypothesis test.

Confidence intervals are also closely related to hypothesis testing. A confidence interval is a range of values within which a population parameter is estimated to lie, with a certain level of confidence. Confidence intervals provide additional information beyond point estimates by indicating the precision and uncertainty of the estimate.

Hypothesis Test Selection		
Characteristic	**Comparison**	**Test**
Test of Mean	Compare Sample Average vs Population Mean (with SD known)	1 Sample Z test
Y is Continuous	Compare Sample Average vs Population Mean	1 Sample t test
	Compare Average A Vs Average B	2 Sample t test
X is discrete	Compare Average of more than 2 groups	ANOVA
Variance	Compare Variance A Vs Variance B	F test
Y is Continuous	Compare Variance of more than 2 groups	Bartlett
X is discrete	Compare Variance of more than 2 groups	Levene
Test of Proportion	Compare Sample Proportion vs Population proportion	1 Proportion
Y is discrete	Compare Proportion of 2 groups	2 Proportion
X is discrete	Compare Proportion of more than 2 groups	Chi-square test
Relationship	Linear relationship exist between X & Y	Correlation
Y is Continuous		
X is Continuous	Linear, Quadratic or Cubic relationship exist between several X & Y	Regression

In conclusion, hypothesis testing is a powerful tool that allows us to validate assumptions and make data-driven decisions. It involves formulating null and alternative hypotheses, collecting data, calculating a test statistic, comparing it to critical values, and interpreting the results. Statistical tests, sample size determination, statistical significance, and confidence intervals are all important considerations in hypothesis testing. By leveraging hypothesis testing, managers can ensure that their decision-making is based on reliable and robust data analysis.

TEST OF AVERAGES

There are several statistical tests available for conducting a Test of Averages, depending on the specific situation and data type. In this section, I will discuss four commonly used tests: 1 Sample Z-test, 1 Sample T-test, 2 Sample T-test, and One-way ANOVA. Each of these tests has its own unique application and provides valuable insights into different scenarios.

1 Sample Z Test:

The 1 Sample Z Test, also known as the Z-test, is used when we have a large sample size (typically greater than 30) and a known population standard deviation. This test compares the means of our sample data with the population mean and determines if the difference is statistically significant.

To conduct a 1 Sample Z Test, we follow these steps:

1. Define the null and alternative hypotheses:

- The null hypothesis (H0) states that there is no significant difference between the sample mean and the population mean.

- The alternative hypothesis (Ha) states that there is a significant difference between the sample mean and the population mean.

2. Calculate the Z statistic:

- The Z statistic is calculated using the formula: $Z = (\bar{X} - \mu) / (\sigma / \sqrt{n})$, where $\bar{X}$ is the sample mean, μ is the population mean, σ is the population standard deviation, and n is the sample size.

3. Determine the critical value:

- The critical value is obtained from the Z-table or by using statistical software. It indicates the threshold beyond which we reject the null hypothesis.

4. Compare the Z statistic with the critical value:

- If the calculated Z statistic is greater than the critical value, we reject the null hypothesis and conclude that there is a significant difference between the sample mean and the population mean.

1 Sample T-test:

The 1 Sample T-test, also known as the Student's T-test, is used when we have a small sample size (typically less than 30) or an unknown population standard deviation. This test is similar to the Z-test but employs the Student's T-distribution to account for the uncertainty associated with a smaller sample size or unknown standard deviation.

To conduct a 1 Sample T-test, we follow these steps:

1. Define the null and alternative hypotheses:

- The null hypothesis (H0) states that there is no significant difference between the sample mean and the population mean.

- The alternative hypothesis (Ha) states that there is a significant difference between the sample mean and the population mean.

2. Calculate the T statistic:

- The T statistic is calculated using the formula: $T = (\bar{X} - \mu) / (s / \sqrt{n})$, where $\bar{X}$ is the sample mean, μ is the population mean, s is the sample standard deviation, and n is the sample size.

3. Determine the degrees of freedom and critical value:

- Degrees of freedom are calculated as (n - 1), where n is the sample size. The critical value is obtained from the T-distribution table or statistical software.

4. Compare the T statistic with the critical value:

- If the calculated T statistic is greater than the critical value, we reject the null hypothesis and conclude that there is a significant difference between the sample mean and the population mean.

2 Sample T-test:

- The 2 Sample T-test is used when we have two independent groups and want to compare the means of their respective samples. This test helps us determine if the difference between the means is statistically significant or if it could have occurred by chance.

To conduct a 2 Sample T-test, we follow these steps:

1. Define the null and alternative hypotheses:

- The null hypothesis (H0) states that there is no significant difference between the means of the two groups.

- The alternative hypothesis (Ha) states that there is a significant difference between the means of the two groups.

2. Calculate the T statistic:

- The T statistic is calculated using the formula: $T = (\bar{X}1 - \bar{X}2) / \sqrt{((s1^2 / n1) + (s2^2 / n2))}$, where $\bar{X}1$ and $\bar{X}2$ are the sample means, s1 and s2 are the sample standard deviations, n1 and n2 are the sample sizes of the two groups.

3. Determine the degrees of freedom and critical value:

- Degrees of freedom are calculated as (n1 + n2 - 2), where n1 and n2 are the sample sizes of the two groups. The critical value is obtained from the T-distribution table or statistical software.

4. Compare the T statistic with the critical value:

- If the calculated T statistic is greater than the critical value, we reject the null hypothesis and conclude that there is a significant difference between the means of the two groups.

One-way ANOVA:

The One-way Analysis of Variance (ANOVA) is used when we have more than two groups and want to compare the means of all groups simultaneously. This test allows us to determine if there is a significant difference in the means and which groups are responsible for this difference.

To conduct a One-way ANOVA, we follow these steps:

1. Define the null and alternative hypotheses:

- The null hypothesis (H0) states that there is no significant difference in the means of all groups.

- The alternative hypothesis (Ha) states that there is a significant difference in the means of at least one group.

2. Calculate the F statistic:

- The F statistic is calculated using the formula: F = (MSB / MSE), where MSB is the Mean Square Between (variation between groups) and MSE is the Mean Square Error (variation within groups).

3. Determine the degrees of freedom and critical value:

- Degrees of freedom for MSB is calculated as (k - 1), where k is the number of groups. Degrees of freedom for MSE are calculated as (n - k), where n is the total sample size and k is the number of groups. The critical value is obtained from the F-distribution table or statistical software.

4. Compare the F statistic with the critical value:

- If the calculated F statistic is greater than the critical value, we reject the null hypothesis and conclude that there is a significant difference in the means of at least one group.

- Using these tests, we can validate claims about measurable characteristics. Whether we are comparing a sample mean to a benchmark, assessing the difference between two groups, or determining the variation among multiple groups, these tests provide us with the statistical evidence needed to make informed decisions.

In conclusion, the Test of Averages is a vital tool in Lean Six Sigma methodology for managers. From the 1 Sample Z Test to the One-way ANOVA, each test offers a unique approach to validating claims about measurable characteristics. By following the step-by-step guide and applying the appropriate test based on the data at hand, managers can make data-driven decisions and drive continuous improvement within their organizations.

ACTIVITY – 10: 2 SAMPLE T - TEST

Case Study 1: An analyst at a chain of departmental store wants to evaluate a recent credit card promotion. To this end, 500 cardholders were randomly selected. Half received an ad promoting a reduced interest rate on purchase made over next three months, and half received a standard seasonal advertisement. Did the advertisement promote reduced interest rate increase purchase? (Refer data: promotion.mtw)

Particulars	Description given in problem	Data Type
Y (Response)	Purchase Amount	Continuous
X (Factor)	Advertisement types – Std & New	Discrete
Recommended test	**2 sample t-Test**	Assess whether mean sales differ significantly w.r.to 2 promotions

STEP	CHECK	Ho	Ha	P Value		INFERENCE
1	Normality **(Anderson darling test)**	Data are normally distributed	Data are not normally distributed	New	Std	Since P value are > 0.05, **do not reject Null**. data are normally distributed
				0.362	0.103	
Minitab Path: Stat>Basic Sttistics > Graphical Summary						
2	Check Variance **(F Test)**	Variances are equal $\sigma^2_{new} = \sigma^2_{std}$	Variances are unequal $\sigma^2_{new} \neq \sigma^2_{std}$	0.653		Since P value > 0.05, **do not reject Null**. Variances are equal
Minitab Path: Stat>Basic Statistics > 2 Variances (select test and confidence interval based on normal distribution)						
3	Compare mean **(2 sample t-Test)**	Means are equal $\mu_{new} = \mu_{std}$	Means are unequal $\mu_{new} \neq \mu_{std}$	0.024		Since P value < 0.05, **reject Null** and infer there is significant difference in mean
Minitab Path: Stat>Basic Statistics > 2 Sample t (assume equal variances)						
CONCLUSION: Promotion is critical to purchase						

Case Study 2: F&B manager wants to determine whether there is any significant difference in the diameter of the cutlet between two units. A randomly selected sample of cutlets was collected from both units and measured. Analyze the data and draw inferences at 5% significance level. Please state the assumptions and tests that you carried out to check validity of the assumptions (Refer data: Cutlets.mtw)

Particulars	Description given in problem	Data Type
Y (Response)		
X (Factor)		
Recommended test		

STEP	CHECK	Ho	Ha	P Value		INFERENCE
				A	B	
1						

Minitab Path: Stat>Basic Statistics > Graphical Summary

STEP	CHECK	Ho	Ha	P Value	INFERENCE
2					

Minitab Path: Stat>Basic Statistics > 2 Variances (select test and confidence interval based on normal distribution)

STEP	CHECK	Ho	Ha	P Value	INFERENCE
3					

Minitab Path: Stat>Basic Statistics > 2 Sample t (assume equal variances)

CONCLUSION:

ACTIVITY – 11: ANOVA EXERCISE

Case Study 1: A financial services organization outsourced their back-office operations to 3 different vendors. The contracts are up for renewal and the CEO wants to determine whether they should renew contracts with all vendors. Vendor with the least transaction time will be preferred. CEO wants to evaluate whether to renew individual contracts or consolidate. CEO will renew individual contracts if the performance is similar (Refer data: Transaction time.mtw)

Particulars	Description given in problem	Data Type
Y (Response)	Transaction time	Continuous
X (Factor)	Three Vendors – A, B & C	Discrete
Recommended test	**ANOVA**	Assess whether Average transaction time of 3 vendors differ significantly

STEP	CHECK	Ho	Ha	P Value			INFERENCE
1	Normality **(Anderson darling)**	Data are normally distributed	Data are not normally distributed	A O.941	B 0.448	C 0.433	Since P value are > 0.05, **do not reject Null**. data are normal
	Minitab Path: Stat>Basic Statistics > Graphical Summary						
2	Check Variance **(Bartlett's)**	Variances are equal $\sigma^2{}_A = \sigma^2{}_B = \sigma^2{}_C$	Variances are unequal $\sigma^2{}_A \neq \sigma^2{}_B \neq \sigma^2{}_C$	0.723			Since P value > 0.05, **do not reject Null**. Variances are equal
	Minitab Path: Stat>ANOVA > Test for Equal Variances (select use test based on normal)						
3	Compare mean **(ANOVA)**	Means are equal $\mu_A = \mu_B = \mu_C$	Means are unequal $\mu_A \neq \mu_B \neq \mu_C$	0.104			Since P value > 0.05, **we do not reject Null**. There is no significant difference in mean transaction time
	Minitab Path: Stat> ANOVA > One way (assume equal variances)						
	CONCLUSION: There is no significant difference in the average transaction time of Vendors A, B & C. CEO to renew all contractors.						

Case Study 2: A hospital wants to determine whether there is any difference in the average turnaround time of reports of the laboratories on their preferred list. They collected a random sample and recorded turnaround time for reports of 4 laboratories. TAT is defined as sample collected to report dispatch. Analyze the data and determine whether there is any significant difference in average turnaround time among the different laboratories at 5% significance level (Refer data: LabTAT.mtw)

Particulars	Description given in problem	Data Type
Y (Response)		
X (Factor)		
Recommended test		

STEP	CHECK	Ho	Ha	P Value				INFERENCE
				A	B	C	D	
1								
Minitab Path: Stat>Basic Statistics > Graphical Summary								
2								
Minitab Path: Stat>ANOVA > Test for Equal Variances (select use test based on normal)								
3								
Minitab Path: Stat> ANOVA > One way (assume equal variances)								
CONCLUSION:								

CORRELATION ANALYSIS

As a Master Black Belt Certified Six Sigma Practitioner, Trainer, Coach, and Consultant, I have witnessed the power of correlation analysis in various domains and industries. It is a valuable tool that allows managers and professionals to gain insights into the relationship between two variables and make informed decisions based on data-driven evidence.

In a Six Sigma project, the primary objective is to improve the quality and efficiency of a process. To achieve this, it is necessary to understand the relationship between the output variable, denoted as Y, and the input variable, denoted as X. By conducting correlation analysis, we can examine how changes in the input variable affect the output variable and identify any patterns or trends that may exist.

The first step in conducting correlation analysis is to gather relevant data for both the input and output variables. This data can be obtained from various sources such as historical records, surveys, or experimental data. It is essential to collect a significant sample size to ensure the accuracy and reliability of the analysis.

Once the data is collected, the next step is to calculate the correlation coefficient, which quantifies the strength and direction of the relationship between the two variables. The correlation coefficient, often denoted as "r", ranges from -1 to +1. A positive correlation coefficient indicates a direct relationship, meaning that as the value of one variable increases, the value of the other variable also tends to increase. Conversely, a negative correlation coefficient indicates an inverse relationship, whereas the value of one variable increases, the value of the other variable tends to decrease.

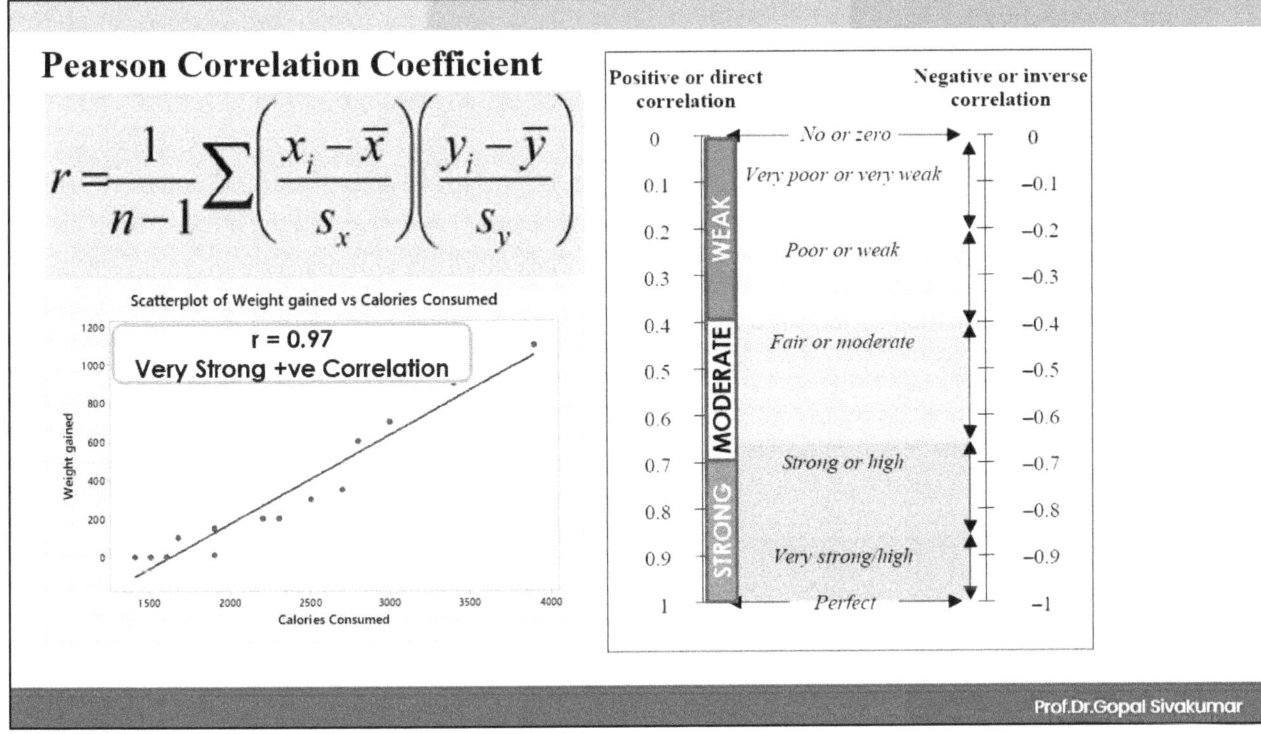

To calculate the correlation coefficient, statistical software packages such as Minitab or Excel can be used. These tools allow for efficient computation and provide accurate results. The correlation coefficient is calculated by dividing the covariance of the two variables by the product of their standard deviations. A correlation coefficient of 1 or -1 indicates a perfect correlation, whereas a value close to zero suggests a weak or no correlation.

Once the correlation coefficient is obtained, it is essential to interpret the results correctly. A correlation coefficient of 0 indicates no linear relationship between the two variables. However, it is important to note that while a correlation coefficient may indicate a relationship between two variables, it does not imply causation. Correlation analysis can only identify the existence and strength of a relationship, but further analysis is required to establish causation.

In addition to calculating the correlation coefficient, it is also necessary to determine the significance of the relationship. This can be accomplished by conducting hypothesis testing, specifically a t-test or F-test, to determine whether the correlation coefficient is statistically significant or occurred by chance. A statistically significant correlation coefficient suggests that the relationship between the two variables is not due to random variation and can be relied upon for decision-making purposes.

Correlation analysis is a powerful tool in Lean Six Sigma as it provides managers and professionals with the necessary insights to make data-driven decisions. By understanding the relationship between input and output variables, organizations can focus on the key factors that impact the quality and efficiency of their processes. This knowledge can guide process improvement efforts and drive excellence within the organization.

One of the most significant applications of correlation analysis in Lean Six Sigma is the identification of critical X's, also known as critical input variables, that have a significant impact on the output variable. By analyzing the correlation coefficients between the input and output variables, managers can prioritize their improvement efforts and focus on the factors that are most likely to yield the desired results. This saves time, and resources, and ensures that efforts are directed towards the right areas.

For example, consider a manufacturing process where the output variable is the defect rate, and the input variables are factors such as machine speed, temperature, and operator skill. By conducting correlation analysis, it is possible to identify which of these factors have the strongest correlation with the defect rate. Armed with this knowledge, managers can develop targeted improvement strategies that address the critical input variables, ultimately reducing defects and improving overall process performance.

Correlation analysis is not only limited to analyzing relationships between input and output variables. It can also be used to identify relationships between two input variables, known as predictor variables. This can be particularly useful when designing experiments or optimizing processes. By understanding the relationship between predictor variables, managers can determine which variables have the most significant impact on the outcome and allocate resources accordingly.

In conclusion, correlation analysis is a valuable tool in Lean Six Sigma for studying the relationship between two continuous variables. By calculating the correlation coefficient and interpreting the results correctly, managers and professionals can gain deep insights into the factors that impact their processes. With this knowledge, they can make data-driven decisions that drive operational excellence and improve overall organizational performance.

ACTIVITY – 12: SCATTERPLOT AND CORRELATION ANALYSIS

Case study: Examine the relationship between Calories consumed (X) and the weight gained (Y). Determine whether the data follow a clear pattern, such as a straight line or a curve.

Weight gained	Calories Consumed	Weight gained	Calories Consumed
0	1500	10	1900
200	2300	600	2800
900	3400	1100	3900
200	2200	100	1670
300	2500	150	1900
0	1600	350	2700
0	1400	700	3000

Minitab Path: Graph> Scatter Plot > with regression

INFERENCE:

There appears to be a relationship between X and Y. Consider performing a correlation / regression analysis to further explore the nature of the relationship.

Correlation Analysis: Minitab Results for: Calories Consumed.mtw

Correlation: Weight gained, Calories Consumed

Pearson correlation of Weight gained and Calories Consumed = 0.970

Pearson correlation coefficient (r) of 0.97 indicates a strong positive correlation and existence of linear relationship

Lower P value (0.000) indicates the predictor variable is significant to the response

$r^2 = 0.97*0.97 = 0.9409$ infers that 94.09% of the variations observed in weight gained is due to the variations made in the calories consumed.

REGRESSION ANALYSIS

When it comes to problem-solving and process improvement, understanding the key factors that contribute to a certain outcome is crucial. Regression analysis helps us determine the influence of these factors on the performance gap we are trying to address. By using this technique, we can identify which factors are most significant and understand how they collectively impact the overall performance.

To begin the process of regression analysis, we must first define our dependent variable and identify the potential independent variables that could potentially affect it. The dependent variable is the outcome or performance measure that we want to explain, improve, or predict. The independent variables, on the other hand, are the factors or inputs that may have a direct or indirect influence on the dependent variable.

Once we have identified the variables of interest, we can then proceed to collect the necessary data for our analysis. This involves gathering data on both the dependent and independent variables for a specific time period or sample size. It is important to ensure that the data is accurate, reliable, and representative of the process or system we are analyzing.

With the data in hand, we can now apply regression analysis techniques to understand the relationship between the dependent variable and the independent variables. There are various types of regression analysis, but the most commonly used is multiple linear regression, which allows us to explore how multiple independent variables collectively contribute to the performance gap.

In multiple linear regression, the goal is to create a mathematical model that represents the relationship between the dependent variable and the independent variables. The model takes the form of an equation, where the dependent variable is expressed as a linear combination of the independent variables, each multiplied by its respective coefficient.

The coefficients in the regression equation provide valuable insights into the sufficiency of each factor in explaining the performance gap. For example, if a coefficient is positive, it indicates that an increase in the corresponding independent variable will lead to an increase in the dependent variable. On the other hand, a negative coefficient suggests a decrease in the dependent variable with an increase in the independent variable. The magnitude of the coefficient reflects the strength of the relationship between the variables.

To determine the sufficiency of factors, we use a tool known as the **coefficient of determination**, denoted as R-squared (R^2). R-squared provides an indication of how well the independent variables explain the variation in the dependent variable. It measures the proportion of the total variation in the dependent variable that can be attributed to the independent variables in the model.

The value of R-squared ranges from 0 to 1, with a higher value indicating a stronger relationship between the dependent and independent variables. A value of 1 suggests that all variation in the dependent variable can be completely explained by the independent variables, while a value of 0 indicates no relationship between the variables. In practice, **an R-squared value above 0.8 is considered acceptable**, although higher values are generally more desirable.

The coefficient of determination is a critical tool in determining the sufficiency of factors for a given problem. By examining the R-squared value, we can assess whether the set of independent variables chosen for the regression model adequately explains the performance gap. If the R-squared value is low, it indicates that the selected factors are insufficient in explaining the variation in the dependent variable, and additional factors may need to be considered.

In addition to the coefficient of determination, regression analysis also provides valuable insights into the significance of individual independent variables. Through hypothesis testing, we can determine whether the coefficients associated with each independent variable are statistically significant or not.

A statistically significant coefficient suggests that the corresponding independent variable has a significant impact on the dependent variable.

Furthermore, regression analysis enables us to identify potential outliers or influential points that may have a disproportionate effect on the results. Outliers can significantly influence the regression equation and, therefore, it is important to identify and address them appropriately.

In conclusion, regression analysis is a valuable tool in Lean Six Sigma that helps managers and leaders understand the sufficiency of factors for a specific gap in performance. By using this technique, we can identify the key factors that contribute to the problem and determine their significance. The coefficient of determination, along with hypothesis testing, allows us to assess the sufficiency and significance of factors, providing valuable insights for decision-making and process improvement. With the power of regression analysis, managers can effectively pinpoint the factors that drive performance and make informed decisions to close the performance gap.

ACTIVITY – 13: REGRESSION EXERCISE

Case study: Is there a statistical relationship between calories consumed and weight gained? If 3300 calories are consumed, how much weight will be gained? (Refer data: Calories Consumed.mtw)

Already scatter plot and correlation analysis confirmed the existence of linear relationship between calories consumed and weight gained. Let us perform regression analysis to further understand the relationship.

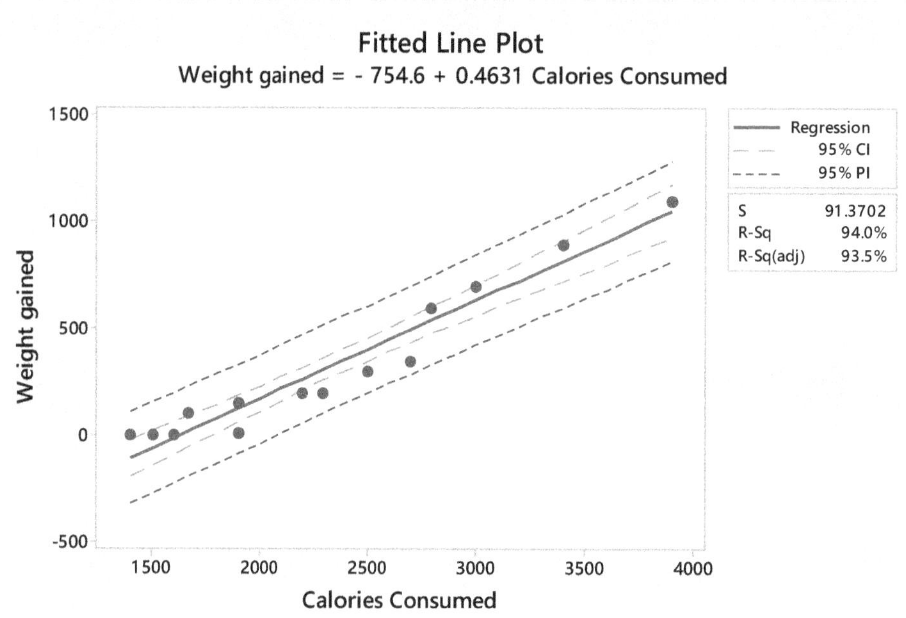

Regression Analysis: Weight gained versus Calories Consumed

Model Summary

S	R-sq	R-sq(adj)	R-sq(pred)
91.3702	94.03%	93.53%	92.09%

Coefficients

Term	Coef	SE Coef	T-Value	P-Value	VIF
Constant	-754.6	82.6	-9.14	0.000	
Calories Consumed	0.4631	0.0337	13.74	0.000	1.0013

Regression Equation: Weight gained = -754.6 + 0.4631 Calories Consumed

VIF Indicates the extent to which multicollinearity (correlation among predictors) is present in a regression analysis. Multicollinearity is problematic because it can increase the variance of the regression coefficients, making them unstable and difficult to interpret.

Variance inflation factors (VIF) measure how much the variance of the estimated regression coefficients is inflated as compared to when the predictor variables are not linearly related. Use the following guidelines to interpret the VIF:

VIF	Predictors are...
VIF = 1	Not correlated

1< VIF < 5	Moderately correlated
VIF > 5 to 10	Highly correlated

VIF values greater than 10 may indicate multicollinearity is unduly influencing your regression results. In this case, you may want to reduce multicollinearity by removing unimportant predictors from your model.

- Regression Line is plotted using the least squares method which minimizes the sum of the squared distances between the points and the fitted line.

- The regression results tell you whether predictor is significant or not. Lower the p-values, most significant is the predictor. Since P value is 0, calories consumed is significant for the weight gained. specifically:

  - For each 1% increase in the calories consumed, the weight gained is expected to increase by 0.4631%.

To predict the weight gained for consumption of 3300 calories, model calculates an expected weight gain of 634.7

CHAPTER 5: IMPROVE PHASE

OVERVIEW OF IMPROVE PHASE

The Improve phase is a critical stage in the DMAIC (Define, Measure, Analyze, Improve, Control) methodology. It is during this phase that the team focuses on generating potential solutions to address the root causes identified in the Analyze phase. The objective is to identify and implement the most effective and efficient solution that will ultimately lead to improved performance and customer satisfaction.

One of the key elements of the improve phase is solution generation. This is where the team brainstorms ideas and alternatives that can potentially solve the identified issues. The team should explore various possibilities and think outside the box in order to come up with innovative and effective solutions. It is important to involve all stakeholders in this process, as their insights and perspectives can provide valuable input and help in generating a wide range of solutions.

During the solution-generation process, tools such as brainstorming, affinity diagrams, and nominal group techniques can be used to encourage creativity and collaboration. The team should also consider the principles of Lean thinking, which emphasizes the elimination of waste and continuous improvement. By applying Lean principles, the team can identify opportunities to streamline processes, reduce cycle time, and enhance overall efficiency.

Once potential solutions have been generated, the next step in the improve phase is solution validation. This involves evaluating the feasibility and effectiveness of each proposed solution and selecting the most appropriate one for implementation. It is important to conduct a thorough analysis of each solution, considering factors such as cost, time, resources, and impact on the organization.

To assist in the validation process, various quantitative and qualitative tools can be utilized. These may include cost-benefit analysis, feasibility studies, decision matrices, simulation models, and pilot studies. The goal is to gather sufficient data and evidence to support the selection of the solution that will deliver the desired results.

After the solution has been validated, the final step in the Improve phase is its implementation. This is where all the planning, preparation, and analysis come together to transform the identified solution into tangible actions. It is crucial to create a detailed implementation plan that outlines the necessary steps, responsibilities, timelines, and resources required for successful execution.

Effective project management techniques, such as project charters, Gantt charts, and milestone tracking, should be employed to ensure that the implementation progresses smoothly and on schedule. Additionally, change management principles should be integrated into the implementation process to address any resistance or challenges that may arise.

During the implementation phase, it is essential to continuously monitor and measure the progress and impact of the implemented solution. This will enable the team to assess its effectiveness and make any necessary adjustments or refinements. By closely monitoring the solution, the team can ensure that it is driving the desired improvements and meeting the defined objectives.

In order to facilitate a smooth transition to the Control phase, the team should document all the lessons learned from the improve phase. This will provide valuable insights for future projects and contribute to the ongoing learning and improvement within the organization. By reflecting on the successes and challenges encountered during the improve phase, the team can enhance its overall effectiveness and efficiency in future projects.

In conclusion, the improve phase is a crucial component of the DMAIC methodology. It plays a pivotal role in generating, validating, and implementing effective solutions to address the root causes identified in the Analyze phase. Through solution generation, validation, and implementation, the improve phase ensures that the identified issues are addressed and significant improvements are achieved. By diligently following the principles and tools of Lean and Six Sigma, organizations can navigate the improve phase with confidence and success.

Major Steps	Step 10: Generate & Evaluate Solutions
	Step 11: Select & Optimize Best Solution
	Step 12: Pilot, Implement & Validate Solution
Important questions to be answered	<ul><li>Does the solution proposed can address the vital root causes?</li><li>Is your pilot study successful?</li><li>Has the solution been effectively implemented and documented to sustain the benefits?</li><li>Has the financial benefit summary been calculated and approved?</li><li>Has any new risk to project success been identified and added in the risk mitigation plan?</li></ul>
Main Deliverables	<ul><li>Selected Solution with Cost / Benefit Analysis</li></ul>

GENERATING IMPROVEMENT IDEAS

When it comes to generating improvement ideas, the first step is to create an environment that encourages creativity and open communication. This includes fostering a culture of continuous improvement in which everyone feels valued and empowered to contribute their ideas. By involving employees at all levels of the organization, you not only tap into their unique perspectives but also increase their commitment and ownership in the improvement process.

One powerful technique for generating improvement ideas is brainstorming. This involves gathering a diverse group of people to generate ideas and solutions to a specific problem or challenge. In brainstorming sessions, there are no bad ideas - it's all about quantity rather than quality. By suspending judgment and encouraging free thinking, participants can tap into their creative side and generate innovative ideas. It's important to have a facilitator who can guide the session, enforce the ground rules, and keep the energy and momentum high.

Another effective technique for generating improvement ideas is benchmarking. This involves studying and learning from the best practices of other organizations, both inside and outside your industry. By comparing your own processes and performance to those of top-performing companies, you can identify areas for improvement and gain valuable insights into new approaches and strategies. Benchmarking can be done through site visits, interviews, or by studying industry reports and case studies. It's important to adapt and translate these best practices to fit the specific context and needs of your organization.

Critical thinking is a fundamental skill for generating improvement ideas. It involves questioning assumptions, analyzing data, and challenging the status quo. By adopting a mindset of curiosity and inquiry, managers can identify opportunities for improvement and explore new possibilities. Critical thinking also involves considering different perspectives and seeking diverse opinions. This can be done through structured approaches such as the "Five Whys" technique, which involves repeatedly asking "why" to uncover the root cause of a problem.

To ensure a successful improvement initiative, it's important to involve employees at all levels in the improvement process. This can be done through cross-functional teams, where employees from different departments collaborate to identify improvement opportunities and develop solutions. By involving employees who are directly involved in the processes being improved, you gain valuable insights and increase the likelihood of successful implementation. It's also important to provide the necessary training and support to empower employees to actively participate in the improvement process.

Building group consensus is crucial for successful change management. When implementing improvement ideas, it's common for resistance and skepticism to arise. By involving employees in the idea-generation process from the beginning, you gain their buy-in and support. It's important to communicate the rationale behind the proposed changes and address any concerns or objections. By involving employees in the decision-making process and giving them a voice, you create a sense of ownership and unity.

In order to foster a culture of continuous improvement, it's important to celebrate successes and acknowledge the contributions of employees. This can be done through recognition programs, employee newsletters, or town hall meetings. By showcasing and sharing the improvement ideas and successes, you create a ripple effect of inspiration and motivation. This in turn encourages more employees to come forward with their own improvement ideas and contributes to a positive and dynamic work environment.

In conclusion, generating improvement ideas requires creating an environment that fosters creativity and open communication. Techniques such as brainstorming, benchmarking, and critical thinking can help in generating a wide range of ideas and solutions. Involving employees at all levels of the organization not only taps into their unique perspectives but also increases their commitment and ownership in the improvement process. By building group consensus and fostering a culture of continuous improvement, organizations can unlock their full potential and drive sustainable success. So let's embrace the power of generating improvement ideas and unleash our collective creativity.

PILOT PLAN AND COMPREHENSIVE FULL - SCALE IMPLEMENTATION

To begin, it is crucial to define project milestones that will serve as the foundation of your pilot plan. These milestones help to break down the improvement project into manageable chunks, allowing for easier monitoring and evaluation. By setting clear and measurable milestones, you create a structure that keeps your team focused and motivated throughout the implementation process.

Allocating resources is the next step in developing your pilot plan and comprehensive full-scale implementation plan. Resources can include personnel, equipment, and time. It is essential to identify the resources needed to successfully carry out the process improvements, ensuring that they are readily available when required. Failure to allocate adequate resources can hinder the progress of the program and lead to delays or even abandonment of the improvement initiatives. Therefore, careful resource allocation is critical for the success of your project.

Assigning responsibilities is another crucial aspect of your pilot plan and comprehensive full-scale implementation plan. Every improvement project requires a dedicated team to execute it effectively. By assigning specific responsibilities, you create accountability and ensure that every team member understands their role and contribution toward achieving the project objectives. Additionally, having clearly defined roles and responsibilities fosters a sense of ownership and commitment among team members, promoting collaboration and synergy.

Establishing performance metrics is vital to measure the success of your process improvements. Metrics such as cycle time reduction, defect rate, and customer satisfaction can be used to gauge the impact of the implemented changes. These metrics provide objective insights into the effectiveness of the improvements and help identify areas that may require further attention. By setting realistic and quantifiable performance metrics, you create a basis for evaluating progress and making data-driven decisions.

However, implementing process improvements is not just about achieving quantitative goals; effective change management and communication are equally important. Change is often met with resistance, and it is the responsibility of managers to address this resistance and facilitate a smooth transition. By incorporating change management principles into your pilot plan and comprehensive full-scale implementation plan, you ensure that the changes are implemented seamlessly, minimizing disruptions and maximizing acceptance.

Communication is a critical component of change management. Timely and transparent communication helps to create awareness, build trust, and encourage buy-in from stakeholders. From the outset of the improvement program, managers should establish effective communication channels that allow for two-way communication. This ensures that feedback is received, concerns are addressed, and progress is shared with all relevant parties. By keeping everyone informed and engaged, managers can cultivate a positive environment that supports the implementation of process improvements.

As you progress with your pilot plan and move towards full-scale implementation, it is essential to continuously monitor and evaluate the outcomes. This involves analyzing the data collected from the pilot phase and identifying opportunities for refinement and optimization. By closely monitoring the progress, you can ensure that the implemented changes are delivering the desired results and identify any potential risks or challenges that need to be addressed promptly.

Iterative improvement is at the heart of Lean Six Sigma methodology, and the pilot plan and comprehensive full-scale implementation plan embrace this principle. Both plans should be viewed as living documents that can be refined and adjusted based on the insights gained during the implementation process. Flexibility and adaptability are key traits for successful process improvements. Therefore, managers must be open to incorporating feedback, learning from mistakes, and continuously enhancing the plans to maximize success.

In conclusion, developing a pilot plan and a comprehensive full-scale implementation plan is essential for the success of your process improvement initiatives. By defining project milestones, allocating resources, assigning responsibilities, and establishing performance metrics, you create a solid framework for your improvement projects. Additionally, effective change management and communication practices ensure a smooth transition and promote acceptance of the implemented changes. With these plans in place, you can confidently lead your organization towards sustainable process improvements, solidifying its position in the market and delivering exceptional value to customers.

SOLUTION VALIDATION TECHNIQUES

1. Multi-voting:

Multi-voting is a decision-making technique that involves selecting the most favored solution from a set of alternatives. This technique is particularly useful in situations where there are numerous potential solutions and the team needs to narrow them down to a few top choices. By engaging team members in voting and prioritizing the solutions based on their preferences, multi-voting helps in achieving consensus and identifying the most viable solution.

The process of multi-voting begins by compiling a list of potential solutions. Each team member then votes independently, ranking the solutions based on their preference. The votes are tallied, and the solution with the highest votes is selected as the primary choice. This technique not only ensures that all team members have an equal say but also helps in avoiding biases and promoting objectivity in the decision-making process.

2. Critical Thinking:

Critical thinking is an essential skill that managers should possess to validate solutions effectively. It involves objectively analyzing information, evaluating evidence, identifying assumptions, and considering alternative perspectives. By applying critical thinking, we can challenge and validate the assumptions made during the solution-generation process.

To effectively utilize critical thinking for solution validation, it is important to ask relevant questions that dig deeper into the proposed solutions. These questions can help evaluate the feasibility, potential risks, and impact of the solutions. Additionally, critical thinking can help identify any potential hidden biases or flaws in the proposed solutions. By actively engaging in critical thinking, managers can ensure that their teams are considering all aspects of the proposed solutions and making informed decisions.

3. Nominal Group Technique:

The Nominal Group Technique (NGT) is a structured brainstorming technique that helps gather and prioritize ideas from a group of individuals. This technique is particularly useful when a team needs to generate a large number of ideas and arrive at a consensus on the best solution.

The NGT process begins with individual idea generation, where each team member independently writes down their ideas. These ideas are then shared with the group, and a discussion takes place to clarify and elaborate on each idea. After the discussion, each team member independently ranks the ideas based on their preference. Finally, the rankings are tallied, and the solution with the highest overall ranking is selected as the primary choice.

The NGT helps in ensuring that all team members have an equal opportunity to contribute their ideas and opinions. It promotes active participation, prevents dominant personalities from influencing the decision-making process, and facilitates the selection of the most favorable solution.

4. Failure Mode and Effects Analysis (FMEA):

Failure Mode and Effects Analysis (FMEA) is a systematic technique used to identify and assess the potential failure modes of a process or solution. It involves analyzing the potential failures, their causes, and their potential impacts. By evaluating the failure modes, teams can identify preventive measures and develop contingency plans to mitigate risks.

To conduct an FMEA, the team begins by listing all the process steps or components of the solution. For each process step or component, they identify potential failure modes, causes, and their respective effects. They assign severity, occurrence, and detection ratings to each failure mode to prioritize them.

Based on these ratings, a risk priority number (RPN) is calculated, which helps in identifying the high-priority failure modes that require immediate attention.

FMEA helps in validating solutions by identifying potential risks and weaknesses and enabling teams to take proactive measures to address them. By systematically assessing and addressing failure modes, teams can improve the robustness and reliability of the solutions.

5. Hypothesis Testing:

Hypothesis testing is a statistical technique used to validate whether a proposed solution has a significant impact on a process or outcome. It involves formulating a null hypothesis (H0) and an alternative hypothesis (HA) and conducting statistical tests to determine whether to accept or reject the null hypothesis.

To perform hypothesis testing, the team first defines the null and alternative hypotheses based on the problem statement and the proposed solution. They collect the necessary data, conduct the appropriate statistical tests, and analyze the results. If the p-value is smaller than the predetermined significance level, the null hypothesis is rejected, indicating that the proposed solution does have a significant impact on the process.

Hypothesis testing helps in objectively validating the impact of the proposed solutions and making data-driven decisions. It ensures that the solutions implemented are based on solid evidence and not just on assumptions or intuition.

6. Process Capability Measures:

Process capability measures, such as Cp and Cpk, are statistical techniques used to assess the ability of a process to consistently meet customer requirements. These measures help in determining whether the process is capable of producing within the specified tolerance limits.

To calculate process capability measures, the team first collects the necessary data on the process performance. They calculate the process mean (X) and standard deviation (σ) and then determine the process capability indices (Cp and Cpk) using the formulas.

Process capability measures validate the capability of the solutions generated by analyzing their impact on process performance. These measures provide valuable insights into whether the solutions can consistently deliver the desired outcomes within the specified tolerance limits.

In conclusion, the validation of solutions generated using various Lean Six Sigma tools and techniques is a critical step in achieving operational excellence. Multi-voting, critical thinking, nominal group technique, FMEA, hypothesis testing, and process capability measures are powerful techniques that ensure the effectiveness and success of the proposed solutions. By systematically validating the solutions, managers can have confidence in the decisions made and drive continuous improvement in their organizations.

CHAPTER 6: CONTROL PHASE

OVERVIEW OF CONTROL PHASE

This subchapter delves into the various aspects of the Control phase, providing guidance on how to sustain the benefits of the implemented solution. The ultimate outcome of this phase is to create a control plan that will serve as a roadmap for the process owner and stakeholders of the improved process.

To begin with, let's understand the fundamental purpose of the Control phase. Its primary objective is to prevent the process from reverting to its previous state and to establish a robust mechanism to monitor and control the process's performance. By implementing effective controls, we ensure that the improvements are sustained and any deviations from the desired performance are detected and rectified promptly.

One of the key elements of the Control phase is the creation of a control plan. This plan serves as a comprehensive document that outlines the actions and responsibilities required to maintain the improved process. It includes detailed instructions on monitoring the process, collecting data, analyzing performance metrics, and taking corrective actions when necessary. By having a well-defined control plan, the process owner and stakeholders can navigate the complexities of the improved process with confidence.

The first step in creating a control plan is to identify the critical process characteristics that need to be monitored. These characteristics, often referred to as Critical-to-Quality (CTQ) parameters, directly impact the customer's perception of quality. By tracking and analyzing these CTQ parameters, we can ascertain whether the process is performing within the desired specifications or if any deviations are occurring.

In addition to CTQ parameters, it is crucial to consider key performance indicators (KPIs) that provide a broader perspective on the process performance. KPIs may include cycle time, defect rates, customer satisfaction scores, or any other metrics that are relevant to the specific process and its objectives. These KPIs serve as a dashboard to evaluate the overall health of the process and provide early indications of potential issues.

Once the critical process characteristics and KPIs are identified, the next step is to establish a robust data collection and analysis system. This involves determining the frequency of data collection, defining the data sources, and establishing measurement systems that provide accurate and reliable data. The data collected should be analyzed using statistical tools and techniques to identify any trends or patterns that may require intervention.

In parallel with data collection and analysis, it is vital to set up a monitoring system that triggers alerts whenever performance deviates from the desired targets. This early warning system can take the form of visual controls, such as control charts, or automated alerts that notify the process owner and stakeholders when specific thresholds are exceeded. By promptly detecting deviations, we can take timely corrective actions and prevent any deterioration in process performance.

The control plan should also incorporate a mechanism for ongoing process improvement. Continuous improvement is at the heart of Lean Six Sigma, and the Control phase is an ideal opportunity to embed this philosophy within the organization. By encouraging a culture of continuous improvement, we can ensure that the process keeps evolving and remains aligned with the changing customer requirements and business goals.

Furthermore, the control plan should clearly define the roles and responsibilities of the process owner and stakeholders. It is essential to have a designated process owner who takes ownership of the improved process and leads the effort to sustain the benefits. The control plan should also outline the roles of other stakeholders, such as operators, supervisors, and quality assurance personnel, who play a pivotal role in maintaining the process integrity.

Regular reviews and audits are another critical component of the Control phase. These reviews provide an opportunity to assess the effectiveness of the control plan and identify any gaps or areas for improvement. The process owner and stakeholders should collaborate to conduct periodic reviews, analyze the process performance, and take corrective actions to address any shortcomings.

In addition to reviews, the control plan should incorporate a mechanism for feedback and communication. Feedback can come from various sources, including customers, suppliers, and employees. By actively seeking feedback and listening to the voices of those impacted by the process, we can gain valuable insights and make necessary adjustments to improve the process further.

Ultimately, the goal of the Control phase is to institutionalize the improvements achieved through the Lean Six Sigma journey. By creating a robust control plan, monitoring the process performance, and continuously striving for improvement, we can ensure the long-term sustainability and success of the improved process. The control plan serves as a guiding light for the process owner and stakeholders, enabling them to navigate through any challenges and seize opportunities to create value for the organization and its customers.

In conclusion, the Control phase is the culmination of the DMAIC methodology, marking the transition from implementation to sustained success. Creating an effective control plan, monitoring the critical process characteristics and KPIs, establishing a robust data collection and analysis system, and fostering a culture of continuous improvement are key elements of this phase. By diligently following the control plan, conducting regular reviews, seeking feedback, and taking corrective actions, we can ensure that the improvements achieved through Lean Six Sigma become an integral part of the organization's DNA.

Major Steps	Step 13: Implement Control System for Critical 'X'
	Step 14: Document Solution & Benefits
	Step 15: Handover to Project Owner, Project Closure
Important questions to be answered	<ul><li>Is there a control plan in place for this project?</li><li>How will input, process and output variables be checked to detect for sub-optimal conditions?</li><li>Are control charts being used? If "No", then why?</li><li>What key inputs and outputs are being measured?</li><li>Has the process been transferred to the process owner along with appropriate Control Plan?</li><li>Are pending tasks, if any communicated?</li></ul>
Main Deliverables	<ul><li>Process Control Plan & Documentation</li></ul>

CONTROL PLAN

One of the key tools in developing a control plan is the control chart. This chart allows us to monitor and control a process over time, detecting any variations that may occur. By tracking these variations, we can take proactive measures to prevent them from affecting the process performance. This helps us maintain the gains achieved through Lean Six Sigma efforts.

Another essential tool in the control plan is poka yoke, also known as mistake-proofing. Poka-yoke techniques are designed to prevent errors from occurring or detect them as they happen. By implementing poka yoke mechanisms in the process, we can reduce the chances of defects and errors. This leads to enhanced quality and reliability, making the process more robust and capable of consistently meeting customer requirements.

Besides using specific tools, it is crucial to document the lessons learned throughout the improvement journey. This knowledge capture ensures that we don't repeat mistakes and can refer back to past experiences when faced with similar challenges in the future. Documenting the lessons learned also helps in knowledge transfer and sharing, enabling others to benefit from the collective wisdom of the team.

Creating updated process flow charts is another key element of the control plan. Process flow charts visually depict the steps, inputs, and outputs involved in a process. By documenting the revised process flows, we can ensure that everyone understands how the process should now be executed. This leads to standardized and consistent procedures across the organization, reducing variation and increasing productivity.

Standardizing and normalizing the revised procedures are integral to maintaining the improvements achieved through Lean Six Sigma. By establishing clear and concise procedures, we can ensure that the process is executed consistently and accurately. This reduces the chances of errors and deviations, leading to improved efficiency and effectiveness.

To successfully implement the control plan, it is crucial to create a culture of continuous improvement within the organization. The team's achievement in spreading this culture should be recognized and celebrated. By acknowledging the efforts and contributions of the team members, we motivate them to continue their pursuit of excellence. This recognition also encourages others in the organization to embrace Lean Six Sigma principles and work towards achieving similar results.

In addition to the tools and techniques mentioned above, the control plan should also address the need for ongoing monitoring and measurement. Regularly evaluating the process performance ensures that any deviations or issues are identified promptly and addressed in a timely manner. This allows us to proactively prevent failures and maintain improved results.

The control plan should also include provisions for feedback and input from employees who work directly with the process. This empowers them to identify potential areas of improvement and provide valuable insights into daily operations. By involving the employees in the control plan, we foster a sense of ownership and commitment, leading to sustained success.

Furthermore, the control plan should outline the process for continuous review and improvement. As the organization evolves and customer requirements change, it is essential to stay adaptable and responsive. Regularly reviewing the control plan and making necessary adjustments ensures that the process remains aligned with the organization's goals and objectives.

In conclusion, the control plan is a vital component of sustaining the improved results achieved through Lean Six Sigma initiatives. By leveraging tools such as control charts, and poka yoke, documenting lessons learned, creating updated process flow charts, and standardizing revised procedures, we can prevent failures from occurring again. It is essential to recognize and celebrate the team's achievements in spreading a culture of continuous improvement throughout the organization. By implementing an effective control plan, we can ensure that the gains made through Lean Six Sigma are not only maintained but also continually improved upon.

X BAR - R CONTROL CHART

To begin, let's demystify some key terminologies. In the context of process control, common cause variation refers to the inherent variability that is present in any process. It is the normal or expected variation that occurs due to the combination of multiple factors and variables that affect the process. On the other hand, special cause variation is the result of specific events or factors that cause an abnormal or unexpected shift in the process. These variations, if left unaddressed, can lead to defects, errors, and instability in the process.

In the aviation industry, where safety and precision are paramount, ensuring control over processes is of utmost importance. For example, let's consider the process of aircraft maintenance, where various activities are carried out to ensure the airworthiness of an aircraft. In this context, common cause variation refers to the normal fluctuations and uncertainties associated with maintenance activities. This variation can arise due to factors such as human error, environmental conditions, or equipment limitations. Special cause variation, on the other hand, may occur in situations where there is a sudden change in maintenance procedures, a breakdown in communication, or an unforeseen external event.

To effectively monitor and control these variations, the X bar R control chart comes into play. This chart allows managers to visually represent the variation in a process and identify whether it is due to common causes or special causes. The X bar chart is used to track the average of a process, while the R chart observes the range of values within each sample. By analyzing these two parameters simultaneously, managers can gain a comprehensive understanding of the process performance.

Let's take a closer look at how to plot an X-bar R chart using a step-by-step approach. Imagine a scenario where we want to track the time taken to complete a specific maintenance task in an aircraft hangar. We have collected data on the time taken for ten consecutive maintenance tasks over a period of one week.

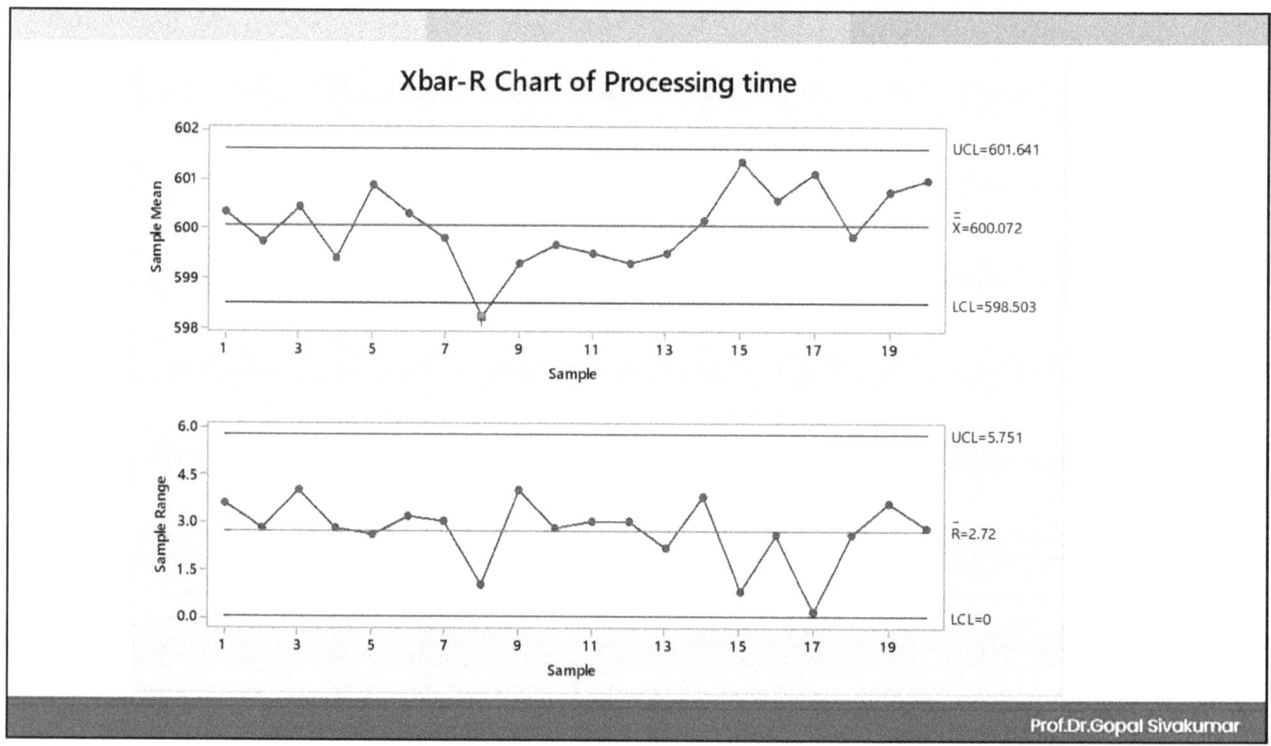

Step 1: Calculate the X bar and R values:

First, we need to calculate the average (X bar) and range (R) for each sample. To calculate the X bar, we sum up the individual data points and divide it by the number of samples. For each sample, we calculate the range by subtracting the smallest value from the largest value within that sample.

Step 2: Calculate the X double bar value:

Next, we calculate the average of all the X-bar values obtained in Step 1. This X double bar value represents the overall average of the process.

Step 3: Calculate the control limits:

To determine the control limits for the X bar chart, we need to calculate the upper and lower control limits (UCL and LCL). The UCL is calculated by adding three times the average of the R values (3R bar) to the X double bar value, while the LCL is obtained by subtracting three times the average of the R values from the X double bar value.

Step 4: Plot the X-bar R chart:

With the X bar, R values, and control limits calculated, we can now plot the X bar R chart. On the horizontal axis, we represent the samples (in this case, ten consecutive maintenance tasks), and on the vertical axis, we plot the X bar and R values. Each X bar value is represented by a point, and the control limits are plotted as horizontal lines on the chart.

Step 5: Analyze the chart:

Now that we have plotted the X-bar R chart, we can interpret the results and analyze the process performance. If all the X bar values lie between the control limits, and there are no obvious patterns or trends in the chart, it indicates that the process is under control and that variation is due to common causes. However, if any X bar value falls outside the control limits or if there are patterns or trends in the chart, it signals the presence of special causes of variation, which warrant further investigation and action.

By following these step-by-step instructions, managers can effectively monitor and control variation in their processes using the X bar R control chart. It allows them to identify and address both common causes and special causes of variation, ultimately leading to improved process performance and quality outcomes. Selection of various control chart depends on data type, and subgroup size and is summarized below.

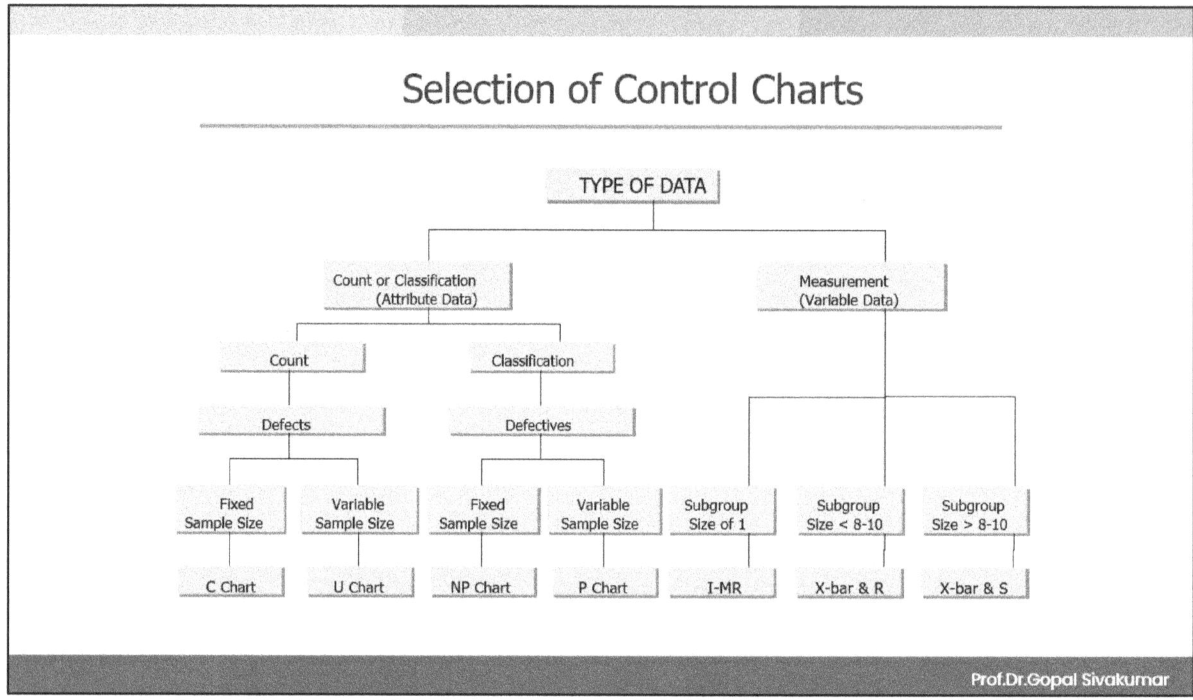

In conclusion, understanding the terminologies of common cause and special cause variation in the context of process control is instrumental in maintaining quality and excellence in the aviation industry. The X bar R control chart serves as a powerful tool to analyze and monitor such variations, enabling managers to take proactive measures to ensure process stability and improvement. By plotting and interpreting the X bar R chart, managers can gain valuable insights into their processes, enabling them to make data-driven decisions and drive continuous improvement efforts.

DOCUMENTING THE PROJECT CLOSURE

1. Project Summary Report:

One of the key documents in project closure is the Project Summary Report. This report provides a high-level overview of the entire project, highlighting the goals, objectives, timelines, and outcomes achieved. It serves as a reference for future projects and allows stakeholders to gain a holistic understanding of the project's success. The Project Summary Report should include a brief introduction, project scope, methodology used, key findings, solutions implemented, and quantifiable results.

2. Lessons Learned:

Another significant document in project closure is the Lessons Learned report. This report captures the experiences and insights gained throughout the project. It serves as a valuable resource for future projects, highlighting both the successes and failures, and providing recommendations for improvement. The report should include a detailed analysis of the project's strengths and weaknesses, challenges faced, solutions implemented, and suggestions for similar projects in the future.

3. Process Documentation:

Ensuring the sustainability of the improvements made during the project requires thorough process documentation. This includes documenting the revised standard operating procedures (SOPs), work instructions, process flows, and any other relevant documentation. The process owner can use this documentation as a guide to ensure the continued success of the improved process. It should include step-by-step instructions, visual aids, and any necessary explanations or annotations.

4. Control Plan:

To maintain the gains achieved through the project, a Control Plan is essential. This document outlines the various control measures that will be implemented to ensure that the process remains within the desired limits. It includes details such as control charts, monitoring frequencies, process checks, and review processes. The Control Plan outlines how the process owner can consistently monitor and sustain the improvements. It should also include contingency plans for addressing any deviations from the desired performance.

5. Handover Documentation:

The successful handover of the improved process to the process owner is a crucial aspect of project closure. This requires preparing documentation that facilitates the smooth transition of responsibilities. The handover documentation should include information such as the project objectives, timelines, key findings, lessons learned, and any other pertinent details. It should also provide a comprehensive overview of the implemented solutions and the necessary steps for the process owner to maintain and continuously improve the process.

6. Stakeholder Communication:

Effective communication with stakeholders is vital in project closure. This involves informing them about the project's completion, providing an overview of the achieved results, and sharing the project summary report. It is important to recognize and appreciate the contributions of all stakeholders, including team members, management, and process owners. Transparent and timely communication ensures that stakeholders are aware of the project's success and can recognize the value of their support.

7. Celebrating Success:

Celebrating the success of the project plays a crucial role in bringing closure to the project. Recognizing and appreciating the efforts of the team members and stakeholders boosts morale and motivates them for future projects. This celebration can take many forms, such as team events, accolades, certificates of achievement, or even a simple appreciation email. It is important to acknowledge the hard work and dedication of the team members, as well as the positive impact the project has had on the organization.

In conclusion, documenting the project closure and providing a comprehensive handover to the process owner is essential in Lean Six Sigma projects. The project summary report, lessons learned, process documentation, control plan, handover documentation, stakeholder communication, and celebrating success are all integral components of this process. By following this step-by-step guide and ensuring meticulous documentation, organizations can not only achieve significant improvements but also sustain them in the long run. The project closure phase serves as a reflection of the hard work put into the project and paves the way for future success.

ACTIVITY – 14: PLOTTING CONTROL CHARTS USING MINITAB

An inspection process checked parts produced for defectives. The total number of parts produced shift-wise and the number of defectives were recorded for 24 shifts. Is the process in control? Worksheet: defectives.mtw	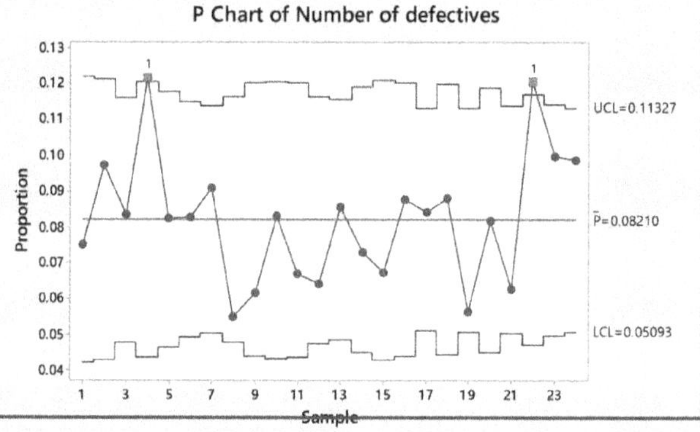 **P Chart of Number of defectives**
A manufacturer of smart phones wants to assess whether or not its process in control. Samples of mobiles were taken every hour for three shifts and tested to see whether or not they work. Defectives are mobiles that do not pass the test. Is the process in control? Worksheet: smartphones.mtw	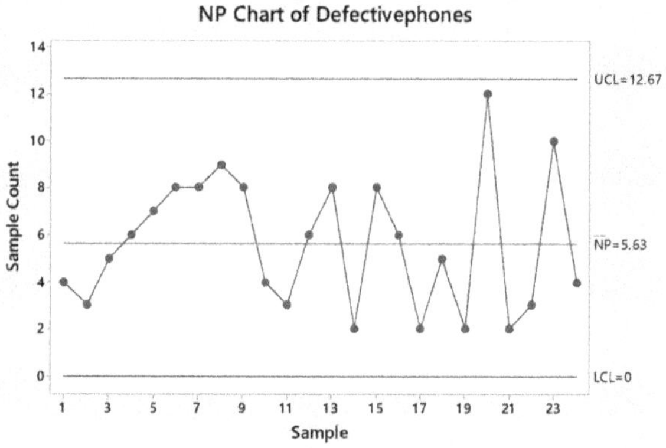 **NP Chart of Defectivephones**
Process excellence team in a bank inspects transaction. There are seven opportunities for error in each transaction. 100 transactions are inspected every day and number of errors are recorded. Is the process in control? Worksheet: transaction.mtw	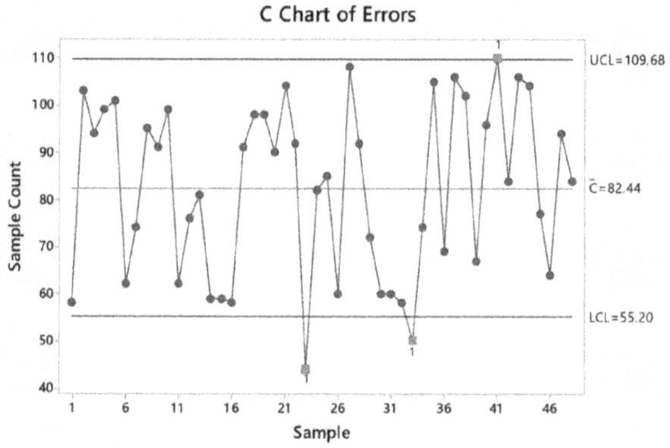 **C Chart of Errors**

<table>
<tr><td>Quality team of a cab company started an improvement project to try to reduce the number of incorrect invoices that is being issued to its customers. The number of incorrect invoices for every day is recorded. Is the process in control? Worksheet: Incorrect invoice.mtw</td><td></td></tr>
</table>

<table>
<tr><td>A pharmaceutical company wants to assess the composition of a particular medicine in a cough syrup and asses process stability. Milligrams of medicine per 10ml in 12 bottles are inspected every week. Is the process in control? Worksheet: medicine.mtw</td><td></td></tr>
</table>

<table>
<tr><td>The purchase order preparation time is recorded for 1 order every day to determine whether the process is in control. Is the process in control? Worksheet: PO processing time.mtw</td><td></td></tr>
</table>

CHAPTER 7: CASE STUDY AND REFERENCE TABLES

DMAIC PROJECT IN A MANUFACTURING INDUSTRY

Title: Reducing Rejections in Sigma Garments: A DMAIC Case Study

Introduction: Sigma Garments implemented a DMAIC (Define, Measure, Analyze, Improve, and Control) project to address the issue of button misalignment in the shirts section. The goal was to reduce rejections caused by this issue and improve overall quality. This case study provides an overview of the project, including problem understanding, CTQ identification, baseline performance, root cause validation, implemented solution, cause benefit analysis, and a control plan for sustaining the improvements.

Problem Understanding and CTQ Identification: The problem at hand in Sigma Garments was the high rejection rates due to button misalignment in the shirts. This resulted in poor quality products that did not meet customer expectations. The critical-to-quality (CTQ) factors identified were button positioning accuracy, alignment consistency, and overall appearance of the shirts.

Baseline Performance: To establish a baseline, historical rejection rate data was analyzed, and the extent of the button misalignment issue was determined. The baseline rejection rate for button misalignment was measured at 15%. This figure provided a starting point for improvement efforts.

Root Cause Validation: A detailed root cause analysis was conducted to identify the underlying factors contributing to button misalignment. Through various statistical analysis tools, such as cause and effect diagrams and process flow charts, it was discovered that the primary causes of button misalignment were inadequate training of shirt sewers, inaccurate button positioning equipment, and lack of standardized work instructions.

Implemented Solution: To address these root causes, several solutions were implemented. Firstly, an enhanced training program was developed to train shirt sewers on proper button placement techniques. Secondly, button positioning equipment was recalibrated and improved to ensure accurate placement. Finally, standardized work instructions were created to provide clear guidelines for shirt sewers, reducing variation in button alignment.

Cost Benefit Analysis: The implemented solutions resulted in significant improvements. Post-implementation data analysis revealed a reduction in the rejection rate for button misalignment to 5%, representing a 66% improvement. This led to substantial cost savings for Sigma Garments, minimizing rework and scrap. Additionally, the improved button alignment enhanced the overall appearance of the shirts, increasing customer satisfaction.

Control Plan: To sustain the improvements, a control plan was developed. This plan included regular monitoring of key process parameters related to button alignment, such as equipment calibration and training effectiveness. Audits were conducted to ensure compliance with the standardized work instructions. In case of any deviations, corrective actions were promptly taken to maintain quality standards. Continuous monitoring of project results allowed for the identification of further improvement opportunities.

Conclusion: The implementation of the DMAIC project in Sigma Garments successfully addressed the button misalignment issue in the shirts section, reducing the rejection rate by 66%. The strategic application of Lean and Six Sigma methodologies, along with the collaboration of stakeholders, including management, shirt sewers, quality control personnel, and equipment suppliers, played a vital role in achieving these improvements. This case study highlights how the DMAIC approach can be employed to systematically analyze problems, identify root causes, and develop data-driven solutions for operational excellence and continuous improvement in manufacturing processes.

DMAIC PROJECT IN A SERVICE INDUSTRY

To address this issue, a DMAIC project was initiated in a call center with the goal of reducing the average call handling time. The first step in any DMAIC project is to define the problem and set clear objectives. In this case, the problem was identified as the **excessive time taken to handle customer calls.** The objective of the project was to **reduce the average call handling time by 20% within six months**.

Once the problem and objectives were defined, a project charter was created. The project charter acts as a roadmap for the project, outlining the scope, timeline, resources, and expected outcomes. It also identifies the project team, which consists of individuals from different departments in the call center, including representatives from operations, quality assurance, and IT.

With the project charter in place, the next step was to establish the baseline performance. Data was collected on the average call handling time over a period of three months. This data was then analyzed to determine the current state and identify any patterns or trends. It was found that the average call handling time was significantly higher than the desired target, indicating the need for process improvement.

To identify the root causes of the excessive call handling time, a root cause analysis was conducted. The project team used various tools and techniques, such as process maps, fishbone diagrams, and brainstorming sessions, to identify potential causes. It was discovered that there were several contributing factors, including system inefficiencies, lack of standardized processes, and inadequate training for call center agents. These findings were documented and used as a basis for developing solutions.

Based on the root cause analysis, several solutions were proposed to address the identified issues. To improve system efficiency, an upgrade to the call center software was recommended. This upgrade would automate certain tasks and streamline the call-handling process, saving time and improving overall efficiency. In addition, standardized processes were developed and implemented, ensuring that all call center agents followed the same protocols and best practices. Furthermore, a comprehensive training program was created to equip agents with the necessary skills and knowledge to handle calls effectively.

Once the solutions were implemented, it was important to monitor the results and ensure that the improvements were sustained over time. To achieve this, a control plan was developed. The control plan outlined the key metrics to be monitored, such as call volume, call duration, and customer satisfaction. It also established a feedback mechanism, allowing agents to provide their inputs and suggestions for further improvements. Regular audits were conducted to assess compliance with the standardized processes, and any issues or deviations were addressed promptly.

After six months of implementation, the project team evaluated the results. It was found that the average call handling time had been successfully reduced by 20%, meeting the project's objectives. Customer satisfaction scores also showed improvement, indicating that customers were benefiting from the shorter wait times and faster resolution of their issues. The success of this DMAIC project not only improved the efficiency of the call center but also enhanced the overall customer experience.

In conclusion, this real-time case study of a DMAIC project in a service industry clearly demonstrates the effectiveness of Lean Six Sigma methodologies in process improvement. Through the systematic application of DMAIC tools and techniques, the average call handling time in a call center was significantly reduced, resulting in improved customer satisfaction. This case study serves as a valuable example for managers in the service industry who are seeking to improve their operational efficiency and deliver superior customer experiences.

TABLE-1: DPMO & SIGMA LEVEL – COMPARISON TABLE

Sigma Level	Without 1.5 sigma shift			With 1.5 sigma shift		
	DPMO	**Yield**	**Defect Rate**	**DPMO**	**Yield**	**Defect Rate**
1	317310	68.2690000%	31.7310000%	697612	30.23880%	69.76120%
1.1	271332	72.8668000%	27.1332000%	660082	33.99180%	66.00820%
1.2	230139	76.9861000%	23.0139000%	621378	37.86220%	62.13780%
1.3	193601	80.6399000%	19.3601000%	581814	41.81860%	58.18140%
1.4	161513	83.8487000%	16.1513000%	541693	45.83070%	54.16930%
1.5	133614	86.6386000%	13.3614000%	501349	49.86510%	50.13490%
1.6	109598	89.0402000%	10.9598000%	461139	53.88610%	46.11390%
1.7	89130	91.0870000%	8.9130000%	421427	57.85730%	42.14270%
1.8	71860	92.8140000%	7.1860000%	382572	61.74280%	38.25720%
1.9	57432	94.2568000%	5.7432000%	344915	65.50850%	34.49150%
2	45500	95.4500000%	4.5500000%	308770	69.12300%	30.87700%
2.1	35728	96.4272000%	3.5728000%	274412	72.55880%	27.44120%
2.2	27806	97.2194000%	2.7806000%	242071	75.79290%	24.20710%
2.3	21448	97.8552000%	2.1448000%	211927	78.80730%	21.19270%
2.4	16395	98.3605000%	1.6395000%	184108	81.58920%	18.41080%
2.5	12419	98.7581000%	1.2419000%	158686	84.13140%	15.86860%
2.6	9322	99.0678000%	0.9322000%	135686	86.43140%	13.56860%
2.7	6934	99.3066000%	0.6934000%	115083	88.49170%	11.50830%
2.8	5110	99.4890000%	0.5110000%	96809	90.31910%	9.68090%
2.9	3731	99.6269000%	0.3731000%	80762	91.92380%	8.07620%
3	2699	99.7301000%	0.2699000%	66810	93.31900%	6.68100%
3.1	1935	99.8065000%	0.1935000%	54801	94.51990%	5.48010%
3.2	1374	99.8626000%	0.1374000%	44566	95.54340%	4.45660%
3.3	966	99.9034000%	0.0966000%	35931	96.40690%	3.59310%
3.4	673	99.9327000%	0.0673000%	28716	97.12840%	2.87160%
3.5	465	99.9535000%	0.0465000%	22750	97.72500%	2.27500%
3.6	318	99.9682000%	0.0318000%	17864	98.21360%	1.78640%
3.7	215	99.9785000%	0.0215000%	13903	98.60970%	1.39030%
3.8	144	99.9856000%	0.0144000%	10724	98.92760%	1.07240%
3.9	96	99.9904000%	0.0096000%	8197	99.18030%	0.81970%
4	63	99.9937000%	0.0063000%	6209	99.37910%	0.62090%
4.1	41	99.9959000%	0.0041000%	4661	99.53390%	0.46610%
4.2	26	99.9974000%	0.0026000%	3467	99.65330%	0.34670%
4.3	17	99.9983000%	0.0017000%	2555	99.74450%	0.25550%
4.4	10	99.9990000%	0.0010000%	1865	99.81350%	0.18650%
4.5	6	99.9994000%	0.0006000%	1349	99.86510%	0.13490%
4.6	4	99.9996000%	0.0004000%	967	99.90330%	0.09670%
4.7	2	99.9998000%	0.0002000%	687	99.93130%	0.06870%
4.8	1	99.9999000%	0.0001000%	483	99.95170%	0.04830%
4.9	0.96	99.9999040%	0.0000960%	336	99.96640%	0.03360%
5	0.574	99.9999426%	0.0000574%	232	99.97680%	0.02320%
5.1	0.34	99.9999660%	0.0000340%	159	99.98410%	0.01590%
5.2	0.2	99.9999800%	0.0000200%	107	99.98930%	0.01070%
5.3	0.116	99.9999884%	0.0000116%	72	99.99280%	0.00720%
5.4	0.067	99.9999933%	0.0000067%	48	99.99520%	0.00480%
5.5	0.038	99.9999962%	0.0000038%	31	99.99690%	0.00310%
5.6	0.021	99.9999979%	0.0000021%	20	99.99800%	0.00200%
5.7	0.012	99.9999988%	0.0000012%	13.35	99.99867%	0.00134%
5.8	0.007	99.9999993%	0.0000007%	8.55	99.99915%	0.00086%
5.9	0.004	99.9999996%	0.0000004%	5.42	99.99946%	0.00054%
6	0.002	99.9999998%	0.0000002%	3.4	99.99966%	0.00034%

TABLE-2: TABLE OF CONSTANTS FOR CONTROL CHARTS

	$\bar{X}$ and R Charts				$\bar{X}$ and S Charts			
	Chart for Averages	Chart for Ranges (R)			Chart for Averages	Chart for Ranges (R)		
	Control Limits Factor	Divisors to Estimate σx	Factors for Control Limits		Control Limits Factor	Divisors to Estimate σx	Factors for Control Limits	
Subgroup Size	A_2	d_2	D_3	D_4	A_3	c_4	B_3	B_4
2	1.880	1.128	-	3.267	2.659	0.7979	-	3.267
3	1.023	1.693	-	2.574	1.954	0.8862	-	2.568
4	0.729	2.059	-	2.282	1.628	0.9213	-	2.266
5	0.577	2.326	-	2.114	1.427	0.9400	-	2.089
6	0.483	2.534	-	2.004	1.287	0.9515	0.030	1.970
7	0.419	2.704	0.076	1.924	1.182	0.9594	0.118	1.882
8	0.373	2.847	0.136	1.864	1.099	0.9650	0.185	1.815
9	0.337	2.970	0.184	1.816	1.032	0.9693	0.239	1.761
10	0.308	3.078	0.223	1.777	0.975	0.9727	0.284	1.716
11	0.285	3.173	0.256	1.744	0.927	0.9754	0.321	1.679
12	0.266	3.258	0.283	1.717	0.886	0.9776	0.354	1.646
13	0.249	3.336	0.307	1.693	0.850	0.9794	0.382	1.618
14	0.235	3.407	0.328	1.672	0.817	0.9810	0.406	1.594
15	0.223	3.472	0.347	1.653	0.789	0.9823	0.428	1.572
16	0.212	3.532	0.363	1.637	0.763	0.9835	0.448	1.552
17	0.203	3.588	0.378	1.622	0.739	0.9845	0.466	1.534
18	0.194	3.640	0.391	1.608	0.718	0.9854	0.482	1.518
19	0.187	3.689	0.403	1.597	0.698	0.9862	0.497	1.503
20	0.180	3.735	0.415	1.585	0.680	0.9869	0.510	1.490
21	0.173	3.778	0.425	1.575	0.663	0.9876	0.523	1.477
22	0.167	3.819	0.434	1.566	0.647	0.9882	0.534	1.466
23	0.162	3.858	0.443	1.557	0.633	0.9887	0.545	1.455
24	0.157	3.895	0.451	1.548	0.619	0.9892	0.555	1.445
25	0.153	3.931	0.459	1.541	0.606	0.9896	0.565	1.435

TABLE-3: STANDARD NORMAL DISTRIBUTION TABLE

Z	0.00	0.01	0.02	0.03	0.04	0.05	0.06	0.07	0.08	0.09
0.0	0.5000	0.5040	0.5080	0.5120	0.5160	0.5199	0.5239	0.5279	0.5319	0.5359
0.1	0.5398	0.5438	0.5478	0.5517	0.5557	0.5596	0.5636	0.5675	0.5714	0.5753
0.2	0.5793	0.5832	0.5871	0.5910	0.5948	0.5987	0.6026	0.6064	0.6103	0.6141
0.3	0.6179	0.6217	0.6255	0.6293	0.6331	0.6368	0.6406	0.6443	0.6480	0.6517
0.4	0.6554	0.6591	0.6628	0.6664	0.6700	0.6736	0.6772	0.6808	0.6844	0.6879
0.5	0.6915	0.6950	0.6985	0.7019	0.7054	0.7088	0.7123	0.7157	0.7190	0.7224
0.6	0.7257	0.7291	0.7324	0.7357	0.7389	0.7422	0.7454	0.7486	0.7517	0.7549
0.7	0.7580	0.7611	0.7642	0.7673	0.7704	0.7734	0.7764	0.7794	0.7823	0.7852
0.8	0.7881	0.7910	0.7939	0.7967	0.7995	0.8023	0.8051	0.8078	0.8106	0.8133
0.9	0.8159	0.8186	0.8212	0.8238	0.8264	0.8289	0.8315	0.8340	0.8365	0.8389
1.0	0.8413	0.8438	0.8461	0.8485	0.8508	0.8531	0.8554	0.8577	0.8599	0.8621
1.1	0.8643	0.8665	0.8686	0.8708	0.8729	0.8749	0.8770	0.8790	0.8810	0.8830
1.2	0.8849	0.8869	0.8888	0.8907	0.8925	0.8944	0.8962	0.8980	0.8997	0.9015
1.3	0.9032	0.9049	0.9066	0.9082	0.9099	0.9115	0.9131	0.9147	0.9162	0.9177
1.4	0.9192	0.9207	0.9222	0.9236	0.9251	0.9265	0.9279	0.9292	0.9306	0.9319
1.5	0.9332	0.9345	0.9357	0.9370	0.9382	0.9394	0.9406	0.9418	0.9429	0.9441
1.6	0.9452	0.9463	0.9474	0.9484	0.9495	0.9505	0.9515	0.9525	0.9535	0.9545
1.7	0.9554	0.9564	0.9573	0.9582	0.9591	0.9599	0.9608	0.9616	0.9625	0.9633
1.8	0.9641	0.9649	0.9656	0.9664	0.9671	0.9678	0.9686	0.9693	0.9699	0.9706
1.9	0.9713	0.9719	0.9726	0.9732	0.9738	0.9744	0.9750	0.9756	0.9761	0.9767
2.0	0.9772	0.9778	0.9783	0.9788	0.9793	0.9798	0.9803	0.9808	0.9812	0.9817
2.1	0.9821	0.9826	0.9830	0.9834	0.9838	0.9842	0.9846	0.9850	0.9854	0.9857
2.2	0.9861	0.9864	0.9868	0.9871	0.9875	0.9878	0.9881	0.9884	0.9887	0.9890
2.3	0.9893	0.9896	0.9898	0.9901	0.9904	0.9906	0.9909	0.9911	0.9913	0.9916
2.4	0.9918	0.9920	0.9922	0.9924	0.9927	0.9929	0.9931	0.9932	0.9934	0.9936
2.5	0.9938	0.9940	0.9941	0.9943	0.9945	0.9946	0.9948	0.9949	0.9951	0.9952
2.6	0.9953	0.9955	0.9956	0.9957	0.9958	0.9960	0.9961	0.9962	0.9963	0.9964
2.7	0.9965	0.9966	0.9967	0.9968	0.9969	0.9970	0.9971	0.9972	0.9973	0.9974
2.8	0.9974	0.9975	0.9976	0.9977	0.9977	0.9978	0.9979	0.9979	0.9980	0.9981
2.9	0.9981	0.9982	0.9982	0.9983	0.9984	0.9984	0.9985	0.9985	0.9986	0.9986

TABLE-4: FMEA SCORING TABLE

Guidelines for assessing the values for Severity, Occurrence, and Detection

Severity Rankings			
Ranking	**Effect**	**Design FMEA Severity**	**Process FMEA Severity**
10	Hazardous-no warning	affects safe operation without warning	may endanger machine or operator without warning
9	Hazardous-with warning	affects safe operation with warning	may endanger machine or operator with warning
8	Very High	makes product inoperable	major disruption in operations (100% scrap)
7	High	makes product operable at reduced performance (customer dissatisfaction)	minor disruption in operations (may require sorting and some scrap)
6	Moderate	results in customer discomfort	minor disruption in operations (no sorting but some scrap)
5	Low	results in comfort and convenience at a reduced level	minor disruption in operations (portion may require rework)
4	Very Low	Results in dissatisfaction by most customers.	minor disruption in operations (some sorting and portion may require rework)
3	Minor	Results in dissatisfaction by average customer.	minor disruption (some rework but little effect on production rate)
2	Very Minor	Results in dissatisfaction by few customers.	minor disruption (minimal effect on production rate)
1	None	No effect	No effect

Occurrence Rankings				
Ranking	**Effect**	**Failure Rates**	**Percent Defective**	**Cpk**
10	Extremely High	> 1 in 2	50%	Cpk < 0.33
9	Very High	1 in 3	33%	Cpk ~ 0.5
8	Very High	1 in 8	10-15%	Cpk ~ 0.75
7	High	1 in 20	5%	
6	Marginal	1 in 100	1%	
5	Marginal	1 in 400	0.25%	Cpk ~ 1
4	Unlikely	1 in 2000	0.05%	
3	Low	1 in 15,000	0.007%	Cpk > 1.33
2	Very Low	1 in 150,000	0.0007%	Cpk > 1.5
1	Remote	< 1 in 1,500,000	0.000007%	Cpk > 1.67

Detection Rankings			
Ranking	**Effect**	**Design FMEA Detection**	**Process FMEA Detection**
10	Absolute uncertainty	No chance that designs control will detect cause mechanism and subsequent failure.	No known process control to detect cause mechanism and subsequent failure.
9	Very remote	Very remote chance that design control will detect cause mechanism and subsequent failure.	
8	Remote	Remote chance that designs control will detect cause mechanism and subsequent failure.	Remote chance that processes control to detect cause mechanism and subsequent failure.
7	Very Low	Very low chance that design control will detect cause mechanism and subsequent failure.	
6	Low	Low chance that designs control will detect cause mechanism and subsequent failure.	Low chance that processes control to detect cause mechanism and subsequent failure.
5	Moderate	Moderate chance that designs control will detect cause mechanism and subsequent failure.	
4	Moderately High	Moderately high chance that design control will detect cause mechanism and subsequent failure.	
3	High	Very remote chance that design control will detect cause mechanism and subsequent failure.	High chance that processes control to detect cause mechanism and subsequent failure.
2	Very High	Very high chance that design control will detect cause mechanism and subsequent failure.	
1	Almost Certain	Design control will almost certainly detect cause mechanism and subsequent failure.	Current control almost certain to detect cause mechanism and failure mode.